THE ULTIMATE OFF-ROAD DRIVER'S GUIDE

Dave Logan

CarTech®

CarTech®

CarTech®, Inc.
6118 Main Street
North Branch, MN 55056
Phone: 651-277-1200 or 800-551-4754
Fax: 651-277-1203
www.cartechbooks.com

© 2022 by Dave Logan

All rights reserved. No part of this publication may be reproduced or utilized in any form or by any means, electronic or mechanical, including photocopying, recording, or by any information storage and retrieval system, without prior permission from the Publisher. All text, photographs, and artwork are the property of the Author unless otherwise noted or credited.

The information in this work is true and complete to the best of our knowledge. However, all information is presented without any guarantee on the part of the Author or Publisher, who also disclaim any liability incurred in connection with the use of the information and any implied warranties of merchantability or fitness for a particular purpose. Readers are responsible for taking suitable and appropriate safety measures when performing any of the operations or activities described in this work.

All trademarks, trade names, model names and numbers, and other product designations referred to herein are the property of their respective owners and are used solely for identification purposes. This work is a publication of CarTech, Inc., and has not been licensed, approved, sponsored, or endorsed by any other person or entity. The Publisher is not associated with any product, service, or vendor mentioned in this book, and does not endorse the products or services of any vendor mentioned in this book.

Edit by Wes Eisenschenk
Layout by Monica Seiberlich

ISBN 978-1-61325-699-2
Item No. SA515

Library of Congress Cataloging-in-Publication Data Available

Written, edited, designed, and printed in the U.S.A.
10 9 8 7 6 5 4 3 2 1

CarTech books may be purchased at a discounted rate in bulk for resale, events, corporate gifts, or educational purposes. Special editions may also be created to specification. For details, contact Special Sales at 6118 Main Street North Branch, MN 55056 or by email at sales@cartechbooks.com.

DISTRIBUTION BY:

Europe
PGUK
63 Hatton Garden
London EC1N 8LE, England
Phone: 020 7061 1980 • Fax: 020 7242 3725
www.pguk.co.uk

Australia
Renniks Publications Ltd.
3/37-39 Green Street
Banksmeadow, NSW 2109, Australia
Phone: 2 9695 7055 • Fax: 2 9695 7355
www.renniks.com

Canada
Login Canada
300 Saulteaux Crescent
Winnipeg, MB, R3J 3T2 Canada
Phone: 800 665 1148 • Fax: 800 665 0103
www.lb.ca

CONTENTS

Acknowledgments 4
Foreword 4

Chapter 1: Preparation 5
Fuel 6
Food and Water 6
Table and Chairs 6
Attire 6
Off-Roading with Pets 6
Safety 6
Trail Access 7
Recovery Gear 8
Personal Items 10
Is Your Truck Ready? 10

Chapter 2: Trail Courtesy 13
Reliability Begins at Home 13
When Nature Calls 14
Using the Airwaves 14
Staying Together 15
Sharing the Trail 16
Heading Home 17
Outdoor Etiquette 17

Chapter 3: Adventures 23
Vehicle Selection 25
4WD Events 25
Where to Begin 26
Overlanding 28
Groups and Clubs 30
Getting to the Trail 36

Chapter 4: Organizing a Trail Ride 39
Tail Gunning 40
Advertising 41
Time to Go 41
Driver's Meeting 42
Herding the Cats 42
Communication 42
Time Management 42

Chapter 5: Driving Techniques for Various Terrain 44
Improve Grip 44
Maximize Articulation 45
Engage 4WD 45
General Techniques 48
Soil Erosion 49
Failed Hill Ascent 50
Bump Steer 50
Use the Parking Brake 51
Mud 52
Deep Water 53
Sand 54
Snow 57
Rocks 58

Chapter 6: Recovery 61
Disconnect the Sway Bar 61
Left-Foot Braking 62
Traction Control 63
Pick a Line 64
How to Get Unstuck 67
Winch Lines: Steel Cable versus Synthetic Rope 74

Chapter 7: Four-Wheel Drive 86
Vintage 4WD 86
Part-Time 4WD 90
Full-Time 4WD 92

Chapter 8: Modern Technology on 4WD Vehicles 93
Anti-Lock Braking System 93
Traction Control 93
Airbags 95
Radar and Ultrasonic Sensors ... 95
Cameras 95
Off-Road Cruise Control 96
Hidden Safety Software 97
Convenience Features 98

Chapter 9: Upgrades 99
Conspicuous Consumption 99
Air Compressors and Tire Deflators 102
Mild or Wild 103
Wheels 104
Tires 107
Axles 110
More Upgrades 110
Interior Protection 119
Rooftop Tents and Skottles 119

Chapter 10: Trail Repairs 121
Fitment 123
Kits 123
Cleaning 124
Critical Thinking 125
Trail Repairs 125
Trail Towing 127

Chapter 11: Communication 128
Frequency Ranges 128
FRS Radios 130
GMRS Radios 130
MURS Radios 131
CB Radios 132
Ham Radio 134
Satellites 135
Emergencies 136

Chapter 12: Navigation 137
Topographic Maps 137
A Map and Compass 138
DeLorme Atlas and Gazetteer Paper Maps 139
Printable MVUMs 140
Guidebooks 141
Google Maps and Google Earth 141
GPS 143

ACKNOWLEDGMENTS

Several people were a big help in the creation of this book, especially Elaine Cooke, Larry and Debbie Bryant, and Jay and Angie Bird. Lane Bailey, Steve Melton, and Heather Lynn worked to get a great cover shot. The Rock Solid Jeep Club and Georgia Bounty Runners 4WD Club were also a big help. All of these folks went above and beyond to help, and I'm grateful.

The following people were also helpful in providing the images in this book: Bryan Ackerman (Truck Hero), Susy Alkaitis (Leave No Trace), Carl Bush, Jason Cooper (Rock Your 4x4), JoMarie Fecci, Brent Galloway (Windrock Park), Brian Godfrey (Method Wheels), Dan Grec (The Road Chose Me), Jealynn Hedzik, Brian Higgins (Tread Lightly!), Sam Houston (Offroad Communications), Alan Josse (SEMA Show), Jamie Longmuir (NJ Jeep Invasion), Matt Martelli (Mad Media), Justin Murray (Smoky Mountain Jeep Invasion), Jim Randall (Warn Industries), Kirsten Tiegen (Rebelle Rally), and Kurt Williams (Expeditions 7).

FOREWORD

Driveways across North America are lined with 4x4 sport utility vehicles and pickup trucks. Sales of off-road vehicles stand at record levels. Millions hold the keys to 4x4s that can tackle the roughest backcountry terrain. For skilled operators, a four-wheel-drive vehicle provides access to an exciting and engaging outdoor lifestyle.

Backcountry adventure is more than following others along a 4x4 trail. *The Ultimate Off-Road Driver's Guide* introduces new owners to the full scope of the four-wheel-drive sport. In addition to driving basics, four-wheeling involves choosing the right equipment for backcountry travel, navigating and negotiating rough terrain, and safely recovering a stuck or immobilized vehicle. This book provides detailed strategies for getting your four-wheel-drive vehicle into remote backcountry and safely home.

Dave Logan is a certified International 4WD Trainer, a seasoned instructor, and a veteran Jeep Jamboree guide. Dave's passion for the backcountry, decades of four-wheeling experience, and recognized trail-guiding ability have established his prominence within the four-wheel-drive community. A member of the elite International 4WD Trainers Association (I4WDTA), Dave shares its principles throughout this book.

Founded by Bill Burke of 4-Wheeling America, the I4WDTA serves as the premier training standard for the sport of four-wheeling. Bill Burke drew from his experience participating in the legendary Camel Trophy event in Africa and many years as a professional trainer. Certified I4WDTA trainers must know advanced techniques for safely negotiating rough terrain, how to free a stuck vehicle under challenging conditions, critical vehicle recovery methods, and how to show respect for the environment.

The Ultimate Off-Road Driver's Guide focuses on safe, responsible, and environmentally friendly four-wheeling. A member of the Tread Lightly! nonprofit organization's board of directors, Dave Logan shares the outdoor principles that will keep our backcountry accessible. Four-wheeling drivers who are aware become part of a broader outdoor recreation community. Driving respectfully, staying safe, and remaining on designated routes helps maintain public support for backcountry motorized travel. Responsible four-wheeling drivers keep our two-track routes and designated 4x4 trails open.

Whether you travel with a group or solo, this is a must-read book. In addition to improving your driving skills, you will learn how to set up your 4x4, perform basic trail repairs, use common backcountry communication protocols, and use navigation devices. Dave Logan's easy-to-follow guidelines will help protect your family, preserve your valuable 4x4, and lead to responsible involvement in the four-wheel-drive community. *The Ultimate Off-Road Driver's Guide* should be onboard any four-wheel-drive vehicle that journeys into the backcountry.

Moses Ludel
Author of *Jeep Owner's Bible*

CHAPTER 1

PREPARATION

The key to having a successful off-road trip is to be prepared. It feels good to arrive at the trailhead confident that you and your truck are ready to go. There are several things to consider before heading out.

We're going off-road, right? A myriad of essential materials to be packed are laid out on the picnic table. Many of these items may seem like overkill until you're stranded or stuck and wishing you had packed them. Take inventory, secure your load, and rest easy knowing that you have what you need to get out of a sticky situation.

Fuel

Four-wheel-drive (4WD) trucks get less fuel mileage when driving in 4WD, so having a full tank of fuel is important for every off-road trip. Occasionally, there will be delays or detours that require more fuel than expected. Having a full tank means having one less thing to worry about.

Food and Water

Bringing a hearty lunch, nonalcoholic drinks, and snacks will make the day more enjoyable. It is a good idea to bring along extras in case there is a delay getting off the trail. An extra bottle of water or snack can be lifesaving for a hiker or mountain biker encountered on the trail who has run out.

Table and Chairs

It's a good idea to bring folding camp chairs and a small folding table. They make lunch stops more comfortable. Kitchen-sized trash bags are useful for packing trash out and for carrying items that have become wet or muddy.

Attire

Dress for the outdoor conditions in your area. A long-sleeve shirt or a hoodie may feel good in the morning or evening when it can be cooler. In the winter, wear wool or fleece as a base layer to keep dry and warm. Long pants can be a good idea to protect your legs from briars and sunburn. Bringing a hat and sunglasses may help in hot, sunny weather.

The ground is usually uneven on a trail. Comfortable, lightweight boots will support your ankles and may prevent a sprain. Traditional hiking boots are not needed because there won't be a load carried on your back. Having a pair of rubber boots along is helpful if the trail is muddy. Packing an extra pair of socks is always a good idea. One of the great things about owning a 4WD vehicle is that there is room to bring extra clothes.

Off-Roading with Pets

If you want to bring pets along, be sure that they're well behaved and on a leash. They'll need food and water, and you should be prepared to dispose of their waste.

In addition, be aware that some state and federal agencies restrict where pets can go. They are generally fine in developed areas but may not be welcome on the trails. The concern is that their running or barking can affect wildlife behavior and their droppings could introduce new diseases.

We all go out in our trucks to enjoy the day with our friends. However, pets need to be under control. They should have fun too—but not at the expense of those around you. Loud pets can scare wildlife away from their food or water source or even mask the sound of a predator. Pet waste can introduce new diseases to wildlife. There is also the risk of injury, and they don't have a veterinarian to treat them.

Safety

Here are some safety considerations to think about during preparation. Many 4WD clubs and off-road events have a short list of mandatory safety items to include.

Bring a first-aid kit and know how to use it. Preassembled first-aid kits are readily available, but one can also be assembled in a plastic toolbox or a storage box. The websites for WebMD, the American Red Cross, and Recreational Equipment Inc. (REI) have lists of suggested items for a travel first-aid kit. Check the expiration dates periodically on perishable items to be sure that they are still effective.

The most common trail injuries are sprained ankles, burned fingers, cuts, insect stings, and poison ivy. These injuries are usually easily treated. The local Red Cross and other organizations offer basic first-aid classes.

PREPARATION

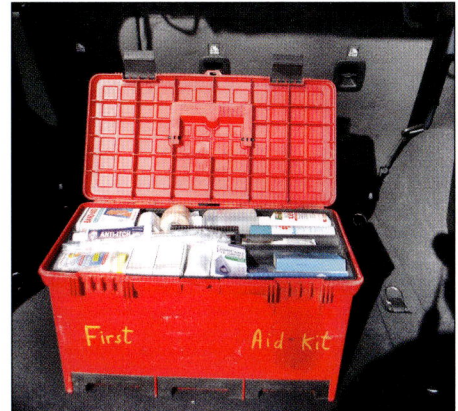

Having first-aid supplies with you can be priceless. They may be needed to treat minor injuries or make someone more comfortable, but certain injuries or illnesses need to be dealt with right away. An allergic reaction, low blood sugar, a heart attack, or a stroke need to be treated immediately. It can be a long way to the nearest medical facility for help.

Basic first-aid kit items include the following:

- Sterile gloves (2 pairs)
- Sterile pads (the thick ones; sizes medium and large that are used to control bleeding)
- Sterile gauze pads (sizes small and large)
- Gauze bandage (Kerlix roll)
- Butterfly closure strips
- Ace bandages (2 inch and 4 inch)
- Triangular bandage (this can be a large square bandana that can be folded)
- Cleansing agent (liquid soap or hydrogen peroxide)
- Alcohol pads
- Hand sanitizer
- Cotton swabs (Q-tips)
- Aloe vera gel (used for mild burns, itching, and to prevent bandages from sticking to wounds)
- Antibiotic ointment
- Hard candy or glucose tablets (for diabetics with low glucose levels)
- Benadryl cream (any anti-itch cream for stings/allergic reactions)
- Band-Aids (all sizes)
- Adhesive tape (nylon or cloth)
- Eyewash solution (saline used for contacts is great)
- Scissors
- Small splinter tweezers
- Instant cold pack
- Ziploc baggies (medium and large) (can be used for ice pack or bloody dressing disposal)
- Aspirin (in case of suspected heart attack)
- Tylenol
- Ibuprofen
- Antidiarrheal medication
- Anti-nausea medication
- Antacid
- Benadryl (in case of insect stings)
- Bug spray

Most people go for years without needing a fire extinguisher, but when one is needed, there is no substitute. When we modify our 4WD vehicles, we often add accessories that need to be properly connected to the factory electrical system. Improper wiring connections or excessive load on a circuit can cause a fire. Don't lose a great vehicle due to faulty wiring or the lack of a fire extinguisher.

If you aren't feeling well, it may be best to skip that trail ride. It can take a while to reach medical assistance in some areas.

Carrying a fire extinguisher can save a vehicle. The basic 2½-pound ABC extinguisher from the local hardware store will suffice. However, it will only last for 10 to 12 seconds. Look for extinguishers with a metal valve and a small gauge that indicates if they are still fully charged.

Be aware that some dry chemicals in these extinguishers can be corrosive, so after the fire is out, there can be further problems in the wiring harness and elsewhere. Halotron is a clean fire-extinguishing agent that prevents this problem, but it is very expensive. Fire extinguishers need to be inspected on the outside every month and inspected or replaced internally every six years. Check the pressure on the gauge periodically.

Trail Access

Preparation also includes learning about the trail or dirt roads that you intend to travel. Internet searches and local 4WD clubs can be a good source of information. State or federal agencies can usually provide digital and paper maps, known as motor vehicle use maps (MVUMs). It's a good idea to call the local, state, or federal agency to get the latest trail or road conditions. It is important to know when they plan trail closures for hunting seasons, controlled burns, and maintenance. Some trails

CHAPTER 1

Planning the trip in advance will be less stressful than trying to figure out where to go while out on the trail. There are many online digital maps and GPS-based phone apps available. However, paper maps and a compass can be very useful too. They allow a wider view of an area and show more routes than can be seen on a digital screen.

Being courteous is one way to help keep trails open for our use in the future. One person's actions can impact everyone. Please pass through public and private land with as little impact as possible. We don't want to let a landowner's cattle or horses out. The gates are open or closed for a reason.

are closed in the winter or may close temporarily due to bad weather.

Paper maps have no batteries or moving parts, but they may be outdated. Global positioning systems (GPSs) and digital apps have also been known to be wrong and mislead drivers. The best option is to go with someone who is already familiar with the trail or area.

When doing research, be sure that it is legal to ride where you want to go. If you intend to drive through private land, get permission. Be respectful and thank private landowners for allowing access to their land. One bad incident with a landowner can cause roads or trails to close.

Remember to always leave gates as they were found. If the gate is open, leave it open. If it is closed, but unlocked, close the gate after passing through. This will keep cattle and horses where the owner wants them.

It never hurts to know the location of the nearest hospital and automotive repair shop. The phone numbers for towing services and law enforcement are seldom needed but are important when they are required. There may not be cellular phone coverage in some places, but if there is coverage, try to call ahead.

It is important to check the weather forecast for the area. Weather can dramatically change a trail's difficulty. In addition, it can affect what you pack, including warmer clothes or extra water.

Recovery Gear

Bringing basic recovery gear is important, and knowing how to use it safely is critical. Having another vehicle as an anchor is convenient and another good reason to travel with others.

Keep the recovery gear within arm's reach so that it can be handed out the window to another driver, if needed. A passenger should also know how to safely use this gear so that he or she can set it up if necessary.

Basic recovery gear typically includes a 30-foot recovery strap or Kinetic rope and bow shackles or soft shackles to make the connection at either end of the strap. Recovery straps and ropes need to have looped ends. Never use recovery straps with metal hooks. The hooks can break and injure someone. The shackles must be rated for the potential load that will be applied to them. Both should be labeled with their working load limits (WLL).

PREPARATION

If you have a winch, be sure to have the remote control, a tree-saver strap, a bow or soft shackle, and a passenger who knows how to hook it up safely. (More information will be given about recovery equipment and its use later in the book.)

A common technique to reduce the risk of getting stuck is to lower the air pressure in the tires when driving off-road. A larger tire footprint increases traction. It helps to have a tire pressure gauge when deflating and inflating tires. It's even better to have a portable air compressor or CO_2 tank. Most convenience stores and gas stations have coin-operated compressors that can reinflate the tires at the end of the trail ride.

A recovery gear kit should include a 30-foot recovery strap and bow shackles or soft shackles to connect the strap between your vehicle and the vehicle pulling you. Having a trash bag to put this gear into after it gets dirty can be useful.

Having recovery gear along is important, but it can't help if it is out of reach when you get stuck. Basic recovery gear should be within reach so it can be handed to a passenger or another driver. Try this at home before it is actually needed.

If you have a winch, it will need the winch controller, a tree-saver strap, and a shackle to connect the winch line. Leather-palmed gloves are required to protect your hands.

Having the ability to deflate and reinflate the tires is important for off-road use. An accurate gauge allows you to adjust the tire pressure to gain better traction on the trail. Too much pressure will give a rough ride and lessen traction. Too little tire pressure lowers the vehicle and can cause the tire to come off the wheel. Owning an air compressor allows you to be independent and not rely on fellow drivers or gas station air compressors. Many inexpensive air compressors are designed to inflate small items, such as beach balls or sports equipment. Large tires and higher tire pressures for street use require a better compressor. Compare the volume of air that the compressor delivers, measured as cubic feet per minute (CFM), and look at how long it will run before it overheats and needs to cool down. This is known as the "duty cycle."

THE ULTIMATE OFF-ROAD DRIVER'S GUIDE

CHAPTER 1

Having spare parts and fluids will help get you home after an unexpected mechanical problem. You can't carry everything, so ask an experienced mechanic who is familiar with your specific vehicle model for the most important items to include.

It is also important to have a full-size spare tire. Larger wheels and tires can be heavy, but when a spare tire is needed, there are few good substitutes. Tire plugs may not always work, depending on how badly damaged the tire is and where the damage occurred. Sidewalls are prone to tears, not just punctures. A jack and a lug wrench are needed to remove the wheel with the damaged tire. Some vehicles come with specialty lug nuts or locking lug nuts. Be prepared in case the lug nuts need a special socket.

Personal Items

Personal comfort items can make the ride more enjoyable, including snacks, drinks, sunglasses, rain gear, and more. Carrying an extra set of dry clothes and a lightweight blanket can be useful, especially with children. Bringing a pair of rubber boots is helpful if you need to walk in wet or muddy areas.

Include a half roll of toilet paper in a plastic bag and a garden trowel. Hand sanitizer is a good idea too. If you are inexperienced with "going" in the woods, learn on your own with privacy and no pressure. The REI website has an online article titled "How to Go to the Bathroom in the Woods."

Having a roll of quarters in a pill bottle is handy for car washes and air compressors when the trail ride is over. Having a spare key that can be reached from outside the truck can save the day.

Is Your Truck Ready?

One of the most important things to consider is the condition of the truck. Is it reliable? There is no roadside service out there, and we don't want to delay our friends to perform repairs that should have been done before the trip.

Unforeseen repairs are needed occasionally, and most people are willing to help, but that requires having the necessary parts and tools to get home. Most organized trail rides will not leave you stranded, but you don't want to make a habit of breaking down on the trail.

There are many ingenious trail repairs that can be done to help you reach paved roads where tow service is available. You will learn as you go.

If you are not comfortable doing mechanical work, then it is especially important to find a reputable automotive shop that specializes in maintenance and upgrades for your brand of vehicle. That shop can usually offer suggestions on which parts commonly fail and the ones to carry with you when traveling off-road.

There are certain parts that will leave you stranded when they fail. It is not practical to carry everything that may fail, so look for signs of impending failure and fix them quickly.

Tools

Most drivers carry basic hand tools. Modern vehicles or vehicles built overseas mostly use metric fasteners. Bolts and nuts may be the same size, so it can be helpful to carry a complete set of metric wrenches and sockets so that you have two tools of each size.

Look your vehicle over. Does it have Torx-head or Allen-head bolts? If so, bring the right tools. An assortment of screwdrivers may be necessary, including small ones. Very few manufacturers use slotted screws anymore, so only carry a few of these. Universal tools, such as adjustable wrenches, wire cutters, and locking pliers, can be helpful.

PREPARATION

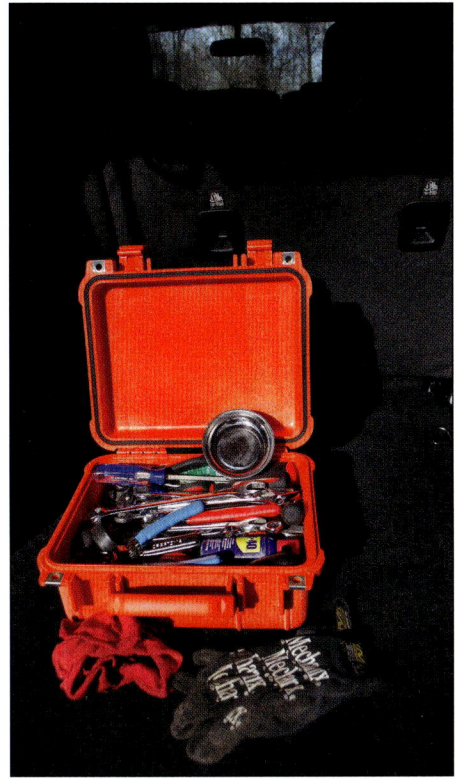

It is a good idea to carry a selection of common hand tools, but you should ask an experienced owner or mechanic about which specialty tools may be needed for trail repairs. Tools can be heavy and require a fair amount of space. Learn what you will need rather than trying to carry everything.

Sometimes the little things become the most helpful. A small camping headlamp allows you to work with both hands. A magnetic tray to hold the fasteners that are removed is a great idea. Once a nut, bolt, or screw is dropped in the dirt, it can be difficult to find.

In general, tools are heavy, so don't go too crazy. Remember that it is only a trail repair, not a major overhaul. Avoid poor-quality tools because they can break. They won't help when you are off-road and miles away from the nearest store.

This is a general list of items that should be carried in each vehicle on a typical one-day trail ride:

Safety

- Fire extinguisher
- First-aid kit
- List of emergency phone numbers for local authorities and tow service
- Cell phone and 12-volt travel charger
- Map of the area (digital and/or paper map)
- Tablet and pen(s)
- Flashlight or headlamp with extra batteries

Wheel and Tires

- Spare tire (full size)
- Off-road jack
- Tire pressure gauge (0–60 psi)
- Tire plug kit
- Air source to refill tires (air compressor or CO_2 tank)
- Lug wrench with correct deep socket
- Special socket for locking lug nuts (if you have them)
- Spare lug nuts (2–3)

Mechanical

- Small plastic tarp to lie on when working under the truck
- Hand tools (We all carry them, but focus on unique tools, a voltmeter, a pry bar, an extendable magnet, and the factory service manual.)
- Common spare parts (U-joints, a fan belt, coolant hoses and clamps, and manual locking hubs if used on your truck, etc.)
- Duct tape, mechanic's wire, bungee cords, and ratchet straps
- Common bolts used on your vehicle (suspension bolts and others that work hard and could fall off or break)
- Engine oil
- Gear oil for the differentials
- Transfer case fluid
- Transmission fluid
- Antifreeze (coolant) and radiator Stop Leak
- Brake fluid and non-chlorinated brake cleaner
- Wire, electrical tape, zip ties, terminals, and spare fuses
- Fluid spill kit (cat litter, a trowel, and a trash bag)
- 6- or 8-gauge jumper cables that are 12 to 15 feet long

Comfort

- Inexpensive rain suit and rubber boots
- Toilet paper (small roll in a plastic baggie) and trowel
- Hand cleaner, hand sanitizer, paper towels, and shop rags
- Trash bags
- Small folding chairs and table
- Ice chest, ice, food, and water for the trip (plus extra)

Recovery

- 30-foot, 2-inch recovery strap with sewn loops
- Two 3/4-inch bow shackles (or equivalent soft shackle)
- If you have a winch; bring your winch controller, gloves, tree-saver strap, and extra shackle(s)
- Small folding shovel

THE ULTIMATE OFF-ROAD DRIVER'S GUIDE

CHAPTER 1

Automotive Fluids

It is also a good idea to carry some spare fluids. Having some engine oil, transmission fluid, brake fluid, power-steering fluid, transfer-case fluid, and gear lube can be helpful. Don't carry gallons of these fluids—just the typical size of bottle on the shelf at an auto parts store. If more is needed, ask other drivers. Hopefully, they have some too.

Note that brake fluid is hygroscopic and will absorb water once the bottle is opened. Partial bottles should be replaced with a full, sealed bottle.

Carefully check the owner's manual to learn what types of fluid your vehicle requires.

Miscellaneous

There are a number of products sold to allow temporary trail fixes. There are Stop Leak products for coolant leaks, JB Weld for temporary metal repairs, Rescue Tape for rubber hoses, and so on. Using these items can get a vehicle back to pavement or even home.

Other useful items include small ratchet straps, mechanics wire, zip ties, duct tape, and more. Jumper cables, fuses, and tire plugs can save the day.

Tarp

Having a small plastic tarp can be a wonderful addition. It allows you to lie under the vehicle and stay off the dirt or mud.

Storage

It is a good idea to measure the cargo space available in the truck and then buy storage boxes or bags to fit. It is better to have several smaller, lighter boxes than one big, heavy one.

It's important to secure storage boxes and bags with ratchet straps that are strong enough to prevent them from moving in the event of an accident. People have been injured by loose gear flying around inside the vehicle. Tools, ice chests, and recovery gear can be very heavy.

Being prepared will remove one source of anxiety. Having confidence that potential problems can be resolved makes the day more fun. That way, you can focus on the trail ride and the people with you. Over time, you will learn more and may even be able to help others.

Securing your cargo can save your life or the life of your pets or passengers. Driving off-road can be very bumpy, and cargo will shift around, but the weight of the cargo is greatly magnified when involved an accident. Accidents on paved roads usually happen at higher speeds and the centrifugal forces and momentum of toolboxes, ice chests, and other gear can be significant. Using ratchet straps that are rated for automotive use is the best solution.

Even with preventive maintenance, new noises or mechanical problems can arise on the trail. A tarp allows you to crawl under your vehicle and look around without getting wet or muddy. When you're done, simply fold the dirty side in and place the tarp in a trash bag to keep your interior clean until you get home.

THE ULTIMATE OFF-ROAD DRIVER'S GUIDE

CHAPTER 2

TRAIL COURTESY

Planning for an upcoming off-road trail ride requires a few important things. Checking the forecast and bringing appropriate clothing and equipment is a good start.

Be sure to have a full tank of fuel and enough drinks, meals, and snacks for the day. Food and drink for any pets needs to be considered too. If daily medications are needed, bring them along just in case the trail ride is longer than anticipated.

Do not bring alcoholic beverages on a trail ride. It is illegal on public trails, and most private parks ban alcohol use due to their insurance clauses. Not to mention that every bit of mental clarity is needed at all times on the trail. Being impaired affects the people and vehicles around you.

It is usually okay to have an alcoholic drink in the evening after a trail ride is over if you will no longer be driving. When in doubt, check with your trail leader.

Reliability Begins at Home

Do your best to perform any maintenance before the trail ride to reduce the risk of a mechanical breakdown. Bring basic tools and spare parts, especially if the vehicle is older or unique.

Make sure to bring all of the "required" gear for the trail ride. As discussed in Chapter 1, a spare tire, first-aid kit, fire extinguisher, and recovery strap are common items that are required. Some organizations may require a citizens band (CB) radio or general mobile radio service (GMRS) as well.

On the day of the trail ride, show up on time or a bit early if you want to socialize or ask questions. Leaving on time is important and helps get the group back on time at the end of the day.

It's fun to have a classic 4x4, but an older vehicle with unique parts requires bringing the tools and spare parts you may need. The odds are high that your fellow drivers won't have what you need for repairs. (Photo Courtesy Pavel Vaschenkov/Shutterstock.com)

CHAPTER 2

It is common practice for an organized 4x4 group to travel on the highway with the headlights on for safety, especially the first and last vehicles. Travel speeds in these groups tend to be slower.

Having privacy when nature calls is nice. Most trail leaders take this into consideration when the trail ride stops. In some instances, it is best to walk ahead of or behind the group. Please leave no evidence behind when you're done. No one wants to see waste and toilet paper.

Turning on the headlights is a common practice on paved roads for safety, but they can be turned off once you are on the trail.

If there is enough room at the trailhead, the trail leader may ask the group to pull over and begin "airing down" to let air out of the tires. Some drivers may also choose to disconnect their anti-sway bars using a button on the dash.

When Nature Calls

This is also a typical time for a restroom break, especially if it was a long distance to get to the trailhead. Privacy can be scarce during some of these stops. Do your best to find cover behind a tree or even between vehicles.

Men have many more options than women. It is typical that women will walk forward or back on a trail to get away from the crowd. You may hear this common phrase: "Men to the left and women to the right because women are always right." The reality is that there may not be a good area along the side of a trail. Briars and poison ivy can grow there.

If you are not comfortable "going" in the woods, a quick internet search will offer videos and other helpful hints. When peeing, please don't leave anything behind. If doing more than that, please dig a hole at least 6 inches deep and bury your waste. A garden trowel is the preferred tool for this.

Using the Airwaves

On the road and when you're on the trail, keep discussions short when using a CB or GMRS radio. The trail guides may have something important to tell the group. They may

TRAIL COURTESY

It is a good idea to practice using the radio before joining a group to be sure it is operating well and that it is not squealing when you transmit. Being able to hear the trail guides makes sure you know what's going on around you. Keep all questions or conversations short so that the trail guides can communicate too.

Trail rides are usually well scheduled to get everyone to dinner or home at a reasonable time. Taking too long at obstacles affects the length of the trail ride and can impact the other people in the group. Ask for help if you need it, but try to keep the group moving.

discuss safety concerns, alert the group of upcoming turns, or need to communicate with the tail gunner (last driver in the trail ride).

It is always good etiquette to not make disparaging remarks about local areas or people when passing through. You are transmitting on public radio channels, and the local residents may not appreciate your humor.

Staying Together

One of the most common mistakes is to not watch the vehicle behind you. This leads to large gaps in the line and can cause people to get lost. If the vehicle behind you slows down or stops, do the same. This keeps everyone together and within sight of each other. In addition, if the vehicle behind you has a problem, you won't have to back up as far to help.

It is also important to wait at turns so that the driver behind you sees the turn and knows which way to follow. Using a turn signal is okay to help indicate which way to go.

To keep the group moving, take no more than three tries at an obstacle. If you can't negotiate the obstacle in the first three tries, ask for a spotter. There is no shame in asking for help to get past the obstacle. The odds are good that others will require help too. This may require use of a recovery strap or a winch, so have your recovery gear nearby.

Trail leaders can only see a few vehicles behind them on some trails, especially if the trail has curves. So, keeping the vehicle behind you in sight is your responsibility. Having gaps in a trail ride can lead to drivers missing turns, especially if there are turns that are close together.

THE ULTIMATE OFF-ROAD DRIVER'S GUIDE

Leave enough space between vehicles on the trail so that the driver ahead of you has room to back up, if necessary. This is especially true on hill climbs. Leaving a gap will also allow space to see the trail and give time to react to obstacles. Tailgating leads to surprises.

Sharing the Trail

Encountering two-way traffic on a narrow trail will require someone to pull over. Generally speaking, the smaller group should pull over. On hills, the vehicle going uphill has the right of way, but trail conditions can change that.

When your group stops, find enough room to pull over and leave a path for other vehicles to pass. It's pretty common for side-by-sides and other trucks to want to get by. When stopping for lunch, leave enough room for other drivers to open their tailgates.

It is very important to use the parking brake every time you park off-road. Trails are seldom level, and there are a surprising number of drivers with stories about their trucks rolling away—especially with kids or pets inside.

A common rule of thumb is to leave the keys in the ignition when stopped. If someone needs to move an empty vehicle, they can. No one will steal a vehicle on a trail ride.

Throughout the day, be sure to collect any trash created. Trash cans can usually be found at the end of the ride or on the way home.

Keep any children or pets under control. Trail rides are typically family friendly, but try to be courteous to the rest of the group. No one wants to deal with an aggressive or barking pet. Kids will usually want to play with other children, but they need to be ready to go when the trail leader starts out again.

Trail access is always a concern. Sharing the trails helps keep them open. We need to get along with fellow trail users and be courteous. One way to do that is to pull over and let others go by. UTVs and motorcycles tend to move faster than 4x4 vehicles. The trail leader or tail gunner will usually let you know when others want to pass.

TRAIL COURTESY

Heading Home

When the trail ride ends, reinflate the tires for safe travel back home. Low tire pressure is okay on dirt trails when traveling slow, but low tires will get hot and can fail at highway speeds. Don't forget to reconnect the anti-sway bar if it was disconnected in the morning.

More than a few drivers have discovered that they were still in 4WD when they reached paved roads. It's a good idea to be sure the vehicle is in 2WD. If the vehicle is reluctant to shift out of 4WD, try backing up a little to release pressure on the gears. Making left and right turns while still on dirt can help sometimes too.

Don't be alarmed if the tires seem unbalanced on the highway. If there was mud on the trail, some may have stuck to the wheels. The weight of the mud can unbalance the wheels. Everything should return to normal once the truck is thoroughly washed.

Modern 4WD vehicles have amazing technology. These features usually rely on a variety of sensors. If these sensors get wet or muddy, they can malfunction. So, don't be surprised if some type of warning light is illuminated in the instrument cluster after a day on the trails. Drive carefully and see if everything feels and performs properly. If so, wash the vehicle thoroughly underneath.

If the warning light(s) stay on, have the problem checked out.

Outdoor Etiquette

The vast majority of people who go outdoors for recreation want to see nature with little or no evidence that mankind has damaged it. In the past, there were fewer people using our outdoor areas. People who grew up in rural settings were comfortable outdoors and were taught to respect nature.

Over time, our population has increased and shifted toward the larger cities. New technology now provides entertainment without ever leaving home. Luckily, we are seeing a renewed interest in the outdoors, but some folks lack the outdoor ethics that were more common in the past.

Today's parents are taking their children camping, hiking, cycling, kayaking, horseback riding, hunting, and four-wheeling. That's a good thing. Lessons learned at an early age can last a lifetime. Both good and bad. Children mimic what they see and hear. The key is not only to teach right from wrong but also to make them care.

The Problem

Unfortunately, we are seeing more damage to our park facilities

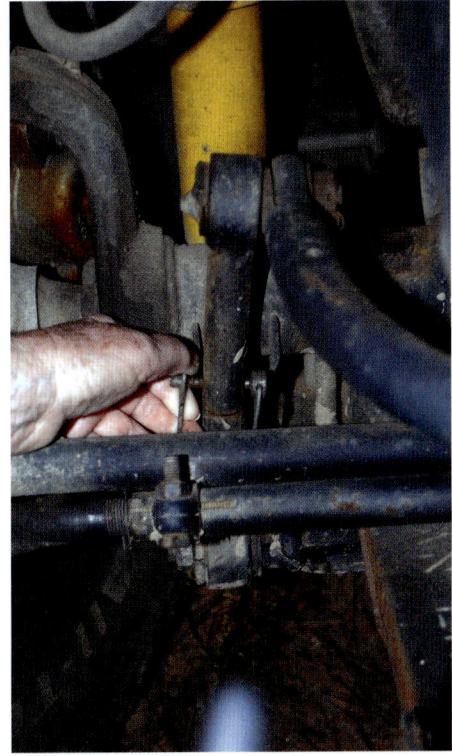

Low tire pressure and flexible suspensions are great for driving off-road but can be dangerous when driving at higher speeds on paved roads. It is a good idea to reinflate your tires and reconnect your anti-sway bar for a safe journey home. Pressure washing mud away from the steering, brakes, and wheels helps too.

Modern 4x4 vehicles have a number of sensors that monitor wheel speed, vehicle yaw, tire pressure, and much more. Some sensors will cause warning lights to illuminate if they get muddy or are knocked out of alignment. If the vehicle is running and driving safely, you should be able to drive it home and take it to your favorite repair shop to have any error codes checked out.

THE ULTIMATE OFF-ROAD DRIVER'S GUIDE

CHAPTER 2

One of the great things that we can pass along to children is the appreciation for nature and the outdoors—the excitement to explore new places and wonder what's around the next bend. There are so many ways to enjoy the outdoors, including hiking, cycling, paddling, riding, or driving. (Photo Courtesy Monkey Business Images/Shutterstock.com)

and trails. Graffiti on boulders and restrooms is becoming more prevalent. Amazing amounts of trash are being dumped at trailheads, and litter is seen on our trails.

The sheer number of people visiting the outdoors is increasing. More rules, regulations, and signs are popping up. Cars are clogging the side roads and parking lots near trails. This overuse creates damage and new challenges for land managers. It also disturbs the lives of the wildlife that we hope to see.

Many of the parking lots, campgrounds, and trails were built more than 50 years ago. Funding to build more has been scarce, and there is a backlog of maintenance for the facilities and trails that we already have. The need for outdoor ethics and respect for nature is needed now more than ever.

The increased level of use also means that we need to respect our fellow trail users. One of the earliest lessons most children learn is to share.

Part of the Solution

Nonprofit organizations such as Tread Lightly! and Leave No Trace were founded in the early 1990s by the US Forest Service to address the environmental damage that was being done on public lands by people. There were few recreational trail systems on public land for motorized vehicles at that time, so people found or created their own trails. Often, this created environmental damage.

Federal and state land managers were late to realize the impact of these motorized trail users, and they didn't understand the hobby. Eventually, high-level administrators in the federal government directed the regional and local managers to designate areas for motorized recreational trails to contain and manage their use.

Respecting nature and the gateways to our trails is important. People travel to seek new experiences or revisit places they treasure. Finding them vandalized or trashed is frustrating. The phrase "This is why we can't have nice things" comes to mind. (Photo Courtesy Ivanka Kunianska/Shutterstock.com)

TRAIL COURTESY

Without clear paths, people will make their own trails, and others will follow those trails. This usually results in damage and a lot of repairs. A well-designed trail system is fun and durable. (Photo Courtesy Igor Bukhlin/Shutterstock.com)

The fact that both Tread Lightly! and Leave No Trace have survived for more than 30 years is a testament to the need for their services. However, it is an unfortunate fact that the need for their services still exists.

The five TREAD principles were written to summarize the overall ethic:

- Travel responsibly
- Respect the rights of others
- Educate yourself
- Avoid sensitive areas
- Do your part

Internal programs were also developed to try and control this recreational use. Eventually, Tread Lightly! was spun off as a stand-alone external nonprofit organization. Leave No Trace followed the same path a few years later.

Tread Lightly! now covers a wide range of activities, but it began with a focus on motorized ATVs and street-legal 4WD vehicles. You can learn more at treadlightly.org.

Many off-road clubs and event organizers have embraced the TREAD principles and practice them in the field. In addition, they conduct training sessions for new 4WD owners.

Tread Lightly! sponsors educational programs for children and adults. It also supports and encourages stewardship projects where volunteers perform trail repairs and cleanups.

"Travel responsibly" means that we need to stay on designated trails. Do not create a spiderweb of bypasses around obstacles or mud puddles. When crossing streams, go directly from shore to shore, if possible, to avoid stirring up silt. Silt can smother aquatic animals living in the riverbed. Driving in muddy areas can create ruts that hold water and cause further damage. Driving though water slowly protects the animals living in the stream and under

CHAPTER 2

The good thing is that when trail repairs, cleanups, or maintenance are needed, volunteers come out to work. Giving back to the places we enjoy is rewarding. Perhaps the best part is the friendships that sometimes form between people working toward a common goal. (Photo Courtesy Tread Lightly!)

It is easy to define people recreating as a "hiker," an "angler," or a "side-by-side driver." However, many folks enjoy more than one hobby. Depending on the season or who is with them, people enjoy a variety of different activities. The angler out in the river today may be hiking a trail with his or her family tomorrow.

TRAIL COURTESY

The seven Leave No Trace principles were written to summarize the overall ethic:

- Prepare and plan ahead
- Travel and camp on durable surfaces
- Dispose of waste properly
- Leave what you find
- Minimize campfire impacts
- Respect wildlife
- Be considerate of other visitors

Knowing what to expect before heading outdoors can make a big difference in how a trip goes. Finding a trail closed when you arrive will definitely change your plans. Being unprepared for the weather can be uncomfortable or worse. Remember that helicopter rescues are expensive. (Photo Courtesy William Booth/Shutterstock.com)

We all go outdoors to have fun. However, having fun shouldn't ruin someone else's day. Startling horses or other trail users doesn't make a trail ride more fun. Eventually, that behavior can cause trails to be restricted or closed. Pulling over or speaking with other people as you slow down to pass makes the day better. (Photo Courtesy GSPhotography/Shutterstock.com)

America is a huge country with a variety of special places. Some of these places are fragile and can be damaged by walking or riding on them. The tracks from our forefather's wagon trains can still be seen in certain areas. Hence the term "beaten path." Some places are historic and deserve protection so that others can see them as they were. Think of these places as outdoor museums. (Photo Courtesy Arctic Photo/Shutterstock.com)

THE ULTIMATE OFF-ROAD DRIVER'S GUIDE

the rocks. There's no need to go fast and spray water.

"Respect the rights of others" means verifying the legal owner of the trail you want to travel. It also means leaving gates open or closed as they were found. Respect also extends to other trail users. Motorized trail users need to yield to hikers, cyclists, and equestrians. This includes pulling over and shutting off engines for equestrians.

"Educate yourself" means doing the research before leaving home. This includes checking the weather forecast and printing or downloading maps. It also means knowing how to drive off-road safely and being prepared for medical or mechanical issues.

"Avoid sensitive areas" such as meadows, lake shores, wetlands, and streams. This protects wildlife habitats and sensitive soils from damage. It can take many years for these areas to heal. Don't disturb historical or archeological sites because they are important to our American culture and can't be fixed or replaced.

"Do your part" means being a responsible adult and role model for kids and other adults. Leave areas better than you found them by picking up litter and properly disposing of human waste. It is possible to still have fun without ruining it for others in the future.

The Leave No Trace organization focuses on teaching people to minimize their impact while enjoying the outdoors. Hiking, biking, camping, horseback riding, and a variety of other recreation all impact the environment. More people recreating means more potential impact. Learn more at lnt.org.

Taking care of the trails and the surrounding land helps to ensure that the trail will still be open the next time you come back. Treating the landowners and other trail users with respect makes life better for everyone. Driving off-road doesn't mean that you can go crazy. Everyone has a better day if you drive well.

We dispose of our dogs' waste, and we should do the same for our own when outdoors. No one wants to see your toilet paper along a trail. It takes no additional effort to carry our trash out, either. Let's make sure that visitors still think of our natural areas as "America the Beautiful." (Photo Courtesy Avanta/Shutterstock.com)

CHAPTER 3

ADVENTURES

Active young people enjoy the outdoors. Many find rugged 4WD trucks and SUVs attractive, and they may find the owners attractive too. (Photo Courtesy LightField Studios/Shutterstock.com)

It is not an exaggeration to say that owning a 4WD vehicle will open up a whole new world. Everyone has his or her own journey. Some folks want a fun "go anywhere" truck or SUV. They may just want a capable 4WD to use for commuting when the weather is bad, while others may want to take dirt roads to reach good hunting, fishing, or mountain biking spots. Many trailheads are located on dirt roads, and a slow scenic drive in the woods can be a good way to escape the "city madness."

Single folks may use it to "pick up" guys or gals. Don't laugh, it works. Some folks want to take the top down and the doors off and cruise the beach. Others build their vehicles purely for off-road use. They may want to race or run mud, rocks, or sand. Where they live often influences how they use their vehicles.

Backcountry camping and overlanding have become popular. People want to escape the cities to experience clean air and quiet nights with a campfire and stars.

Whatever the goal, there is a 4WD truck or SUV for it. Buying the vehicle is just the start. Personalizing it to your needs and taste can be a fun project too.

There are few things as much fun as cruising down a beach slowly with the soft top down and the doors off. The warm, salty breeze takes you away from routine life back home. (Photo Courtesy RudenkoStudio/Shutterstock.com)

While many owners ask their vehicles to multitask, others build them for a single purpose without compromises. Modifying a vehicle will make certain things better but often at the expense of others. Big tires may offer greater ground clearance, but they effectively change gear ratios and require more torque to accelerate. Steering, braking, and other changes will happen as a result of that one modification. (Photo Courtesy Martin Smith/Shutterstock.com)

As cities grow and the population increases, we sometimes look for an escape from the traffic, noise, and stress. Taking the 4WD truck out for a weekend or longer can offer that outlet. Keep it simple and take the basic necessities or go crazy and take gourmet food to prepare under the stars. Just don't forget about the bears. They aren't picky, but they are hungry. (Photo Courtesy Milan Rademakers/Shutterstock.com)

ADVENTURES

Vehicle Selection

A common question is, "What is the best 4WD vehicle for what I want to do?" The answer is, "It depends." There will always be a bigger, badder, and more expensive off-roader to buy. Use your current 4WD truck or SUV to learn what features you want or need. The "want" list is usually long and expensive. The "need" list is usually shorter.

Keep in mind that modified 4WD vehicles and their accessories are not investments. They will lose value over time, especially if they are actually taken out and used. That $1,000 bumper will only be worth $700 once it's been used. Wheels get scratched, tires become worn, paint gets scratches, etc.

One theory is to start by looking for a complete vehicle that has the modifications that you think you want. None will be a perfect fit, but try to get close. Be extremely careful when researching a used vehicle's condition and history. "Buyer beware" is especially true for off-road vehicles.

The alternative is to buy a brand-new vehicle and pay full retail for all kinds of accessories. It's expensive, but everything is new and reliable. The monthly payments may be high, but at least you'll know how much they will be.

Off-road events are a fun way to see other 4WDs, meet vendors, and people watch. It will open your horizons and make you want to spend money on your truck.

4WD Events

To find ideas about certain vehicles or accessories, you can often see hundreds or thousands of 4WDs at events. There are countless off-road

Lifestyle events are usually about brand loyalty. They may be a Jeep show or a Toyota gathering. It's a chance to be among thousands of likeminded people who overlook their brand's flaws and take pride in ownership. It's like a cult without the stigma. (Photo Courtesy Great Smoky Mountain Jeep Invasion)

THE ULTIMATE OFF-ROAD DRIVER'S GUIDE

CHAPTER 3

Vintage events are a chance to see what your parents or grandparents drove back in their day. Some of these events are for military vehicles, while others focus on a particular brand. Historic Jeeps, Broncos, Land Cruisers, or Land Rovers will be on display. Owners have a variety of reasons for owning them. Some 4WDs may have belonged to their family, others remember them from their youth and want to have them again, and some people just like to tinker on simple old vehicles as a hobby. (Photo Courtesy Betto Rodrigues/Shutterstock.com)

Human beings enjoy socializing, especially with a common interest. If you go to a 4WD trail ride or camping trip, you will meet nice people out to enjoy the day or weekend. You may not remember their names, but you will usually remember what they drive. You will almost never hear about their careers or other things from their Monday-through-Friday life. (Photo Courtesy fboudrias/Shutterstock.com)

events. Some include man-made obstacle courses, while others have trail rides. Some are races.

These 4WD lifestyle events provide the opportunity to wander up and down rows of modified 4WDs to get ideas. Swap meets and vendors are common at these shows, and they can draw huge crowds.

There are also vintage events for old Jeeps, Toyotas, and Land Rovers. Military vehicle shows also have a following. These vehicles are a throwback to simpler times and bring back memories for some people.

Who Will You Meet?

There are online 4WD groups and social clubs that meet each month. Each has virtues and a community of people. Some are very broad in their scope, while others are very focused on one brand or activity. While we all love our vehicles, it's the people that make off-roading fun. Don't underestimate the joy in making good friends.

Eventually, you'll find your tribe and enjoy their company. They'll laugh when you make mistakes and then help you fix them. Campfire stories become epic. Never take for granted the time spent with family and friends. You're making memories for you and for them.

Where to Begin

To see what other people have done with their truck or SUV, go to a "lifestyle" event. There are a lot of other people wandering around doing the same thing. You'll discover all kinds of ideas and usually vendors selling accessories. Some may even have a "show special" discount. Attendance at these events can range from a few hundred people to 70,000.

Attending one of these events can feel like the circus came to town. Some people caravan together to reach the event. There are all kinds of activities for kids and adults. The food concessions will rival a county fair. New and used parts may be available at discounted prices, and the accessory representatives can answer most questions. The latest accessories are available in person. Some shows have hourly or daily raffles for prizes. Man-made obstacle courses are a popular activity too. Many times, an event will have a "Show and Shine" area for people to display their best 4WD vehicles. Typically, there is something for everyone. (Photo Courtesy Rugged Ridge/Truck Hero)

There may be a parade, a concert, a man-made obstacle course, food trucks, or even a raffle with prizes. Examples of this style event are Jeep Beach, NJ Jeep Invasion, Toledo Jeep Fest, Bantam Jeep Heritage Festival, Smoky Mountain Jeep Invasion, and Off-Road Expo. There are too many to list them all.

Other events are held in more rural areas, where off-road trails are nearby. This provides a chance to see new scenery or experience more difficult challenges with a trail leader and guides who can offer help. This style of organized event is more focused on driving the trails. Examples include Jeep Jamboree events, All 4 Fun, Silver Lake Sand Dunes Jeep Invasion, Cal4Wheel events, Toyota Land Cruiser Association (TLCA) events, CruiserFest, Easter Jeep Safari, and more.

There are competitions and races as well. There is everything imaginable available. Mud bogs, sand races, hill climbs, desert races, and

Trail-oriented events are a wonderful way to see new places with the security of having trail guides with local knowledge. The trail guides know the trail's condition, difficulty, and where it goes. Having help if you need it is reassuring too. These events usually charge a fee, but a portion of that money may support a charity and the rest often goes toward covering expenses, insurance, and land use permits. Camping may be offered as well.

CHAPTER 3

While off-road racing on racetracks is popular, there are several other forms of competition that people enjoy with their 4WD trucks or buggies. Hill-climbing competitions, mud course races, off-road desert races, sand drag races, and navigational rallies are all exciting options in which to participate or watch. (Photo Courtesy Anthony Alaniz/Shutterstock.com)

Prior to World War II, the US Army primarily used trains and horses to carry troops. Most soldiers walked. However, the US military was testing 4WD prototype military vehicles in 1940 and 1941. "Scout cars," trucks, ambulances, and tanks were ordered, and fleets of vehicles were built all throughout the war. New generations of these vehicles were built during each war after that. Military vehicle shows are popular with veterans and civilians alike. (Photo Courtesy angellodeco/Shutterstock.com)

navigation rallies. Each activity has a unique type of vehicle.

There are also military vehicle shows. The Military Vehicle Preservation Association (MVPA) has state clubs, convoys, and an annual convention. The association has a wealth of information and classified ads. While many people know that Willys and Ford produced the "jeeps" used in World War II, some may not realize that Chevrolet and Dodge produced 4WD trucks too.

Willys also produced military "jeeps" during the Korean and Vietnam wars. After that, Dodge and Chevrolet produced militarized pickup trucks for the armed services.

Overlanding

Recently, backcountry camping has become popular. People may go out alone or they may travel with a small group of friends. Usually, these trips only last a few days. The goal for some people is to travel as far as they can on dirt roads with minimal pavement. Cross-state "traverses" are sometimes held.

Backcountry camping is a popular activity. Some may call it "overlanding," but most Americans stay in America (they don't travel great distances over long periods of time to experience foreign cultures). There are so many beautiful places to explore in the United States that most drivers remain here. (Photo Courtesy xuanhuongho/Shutterstock.com)

ADVENTURES

Camping in remote areas has been getting harder to do in recent years. More and more people are searching for the same experience. At times, solitude is hard to find. In addition, not everyone has good outdoor ethics. Litter, human waste, loud music, fireworks, and excessive drinking are being seen more and more as city dwellers arrive not knowing what is acceptable and what is not. Courtesy is becoming a scarce commodity. (Photo Courtesy GaroManjikian/Shutterstock.com)

Dan Grec is continuing a long history of overlanding. He recently spent nearly three years on the road exploring Africa and came away with a lifetime of experiences. (Photo Courtesy Dan Grec/The Road Chose Me)

Expeditions 7 was an epic journey that covered all seven continents over a three-year period. Greg Miller and his family, Scott Brady, Kurt Williams, Chris Collard, and a list of other notable adventurers participated. (Photo Courtesy Expeditions 7)

Groups and Clubs

When starting out, it is a good idea to join local clubs or Facebook groups. The people in them have gone through the same process. These are also good places to meet some great people.

The term "overlanding" has been used or misused by Americans. The good folks over at *Overland Journal* have defined overlanding as *"vehicle-supported, self-reliant adventure travel, typically exploring remote locations, and interacting with other cultures."*

People who enjoy true overlanding often cross international borders and explore areas using their personal 4WD vehicles. There is a long list of great people who have traveled around the world for months and even years at a time.

After World War II, Ben Carlin, Helen and Frank Schreider, and Lionel Force converted surplus Ford GPAs into oceangoing vessels for extended travels.

There are interesting sagas of people traveling around Africa by Jeep. An internet search will find a book written by two female university professors named Dorothy Rogers and Louise Ostberg, who drove 25,000 miles in Africa in the 1950s using a Willys 4WD station wagon.

Perk Perkins and a friend circumnavigated the world in a Jeep CJ-5 in the 1970s before becoming the CEO of the Orvis Company. His tale can be found in *Around the World in a Jeep*. Mark A. Smith, founder of the Jeep Jamboree USA program, led a 21,000-mile expedition from Tierra del Fuego, Chile, to Prudhoe Bay, Alaska, in 1978 with six Jeeps. It became known as the "Expedicion de las Americas."

Have fun picking and outfitting your 4WD truck or SUV, but the real goal is to explore the beauty of America that few ever see and connect with people along the way. That's what you'll remember most. (Photo Courtesy Ogletree Photography/Shutterstock.com)

Dispersed camping spreads out human impact. The key to keeping this privilege is to not do visible damage. If the area experiences damage, it may be closed the next time. (Photo Courtesy Monica Garza 73/Shutterstock.com)

ADVENTURES

There are still fragile remains of the "Old West" if you explore carefully. However, there are few secret places left due to the internet. Some historic places are preserved, and others are simply protected. Each year they deteriorate a little. (Photo Courtesy Zack Frank/Shutterstock.com)

The general rule is to camp 200 feet away from any water source. Random trail blazing is not allowed. It kills the plants and scares the wildlife. It also compresses the soil, leaving tracks that are visible for many years. Please do not chop down trees or ruin historic places with graffiti.

Some groups explore old mining and ghost towns. In this case, a stock high-clearance 4WD truck or SUV will usually get you to where you want to go. Exploring the history of the Old West is the attraction.

There are certain off-road trails that have become famous over the years either for their scenery or their difficulty. A few have both. The more vehicles that use the trails, the more difficult they usually become. Rocks move and soil is either washed or blown away.

The list is truly endless, and there are many awesome trips to learn about. While preparation and solidly built vehicles are critical, in the end, it's the people, the scenery, and the experiences that make lasting memories.

Be aware that "dry camping" beyond traditional campgrounds is usually considered "dispersed camping" by state and federal agencies. These agencies may require reserving a permit and checking in with them to better manage the land and prevent overcrowding.

Dispersed camping means being self-contained. No services are provided, such as water, restrooms, or trash cans. Check for campfire restrictions if it is a dry season. Look at the Tread Lightly! website for responsible camping ideas.

You can find places to camp on the side of a main road or follow a forest dirt road to a more remote site.

The High Sierra mountains of northern California are a special place. The granite rocks can be massive, and the scenery is special. Off-highway vehicle (OHV) trails, such as the Rubicon, Fordyce Creek, and Dusy-Ershim have wide panoramas, thick forests, and cold alpine lakes. The clear blue skies seem within reach at 10,000 feet. (Photo Courtesy Monica Garza 73/Shutterstock.com)

THE ULTIMATE OFF-ROAD DRIVER'S GUIDE

CHAPTER 3

The eastern and midwestern parts of the United States have fewer trails and more people. Many of the larger cities are there. As the cities developed, very little land was saved for public recreation.

However, as pioneers and early settlers moved farther west, vast tracts of land were kept intact. To this day, many of our most beautiful trails are in the West. The Rubicon Trail in northern California is very well known and is a bucket-list trail for many people. The nearby Fordyce Creek Trail and the Dusy-Ershim Trail are fun as well.

Out West

Southern California has the Anza-Borrego Desert and Death Valley Trails, which offer low-elevation desert scenery. In addition, there are nine state-owned trail systems in the state vehicular recreation areas (SVRAs) throughout the state.

Utah is a unique state with rare beauty. That's why there are 5 national parks and 43 state parks. About 66 percent of Utah's land is set aside for public use. Recreational trail riding can be found within some of the national and state parks. The sandstone found in much of Utah provides incredible traction. It is like driving on sandpaper. However, it is also unforgiving to mechanical systems. You are more likely to find your vehicle's weak link here. U-joints are a common failure. Steering systems are also taxed while trying to turn large, grippy tires on coarse rocks.

California had the foresight to protect and preserve public lands for recreational use. Coastal parks allow people to have beach access and camping. State vehicular recreation areas (SVRAs) allow off-highway riders and drivers to enjoy the unique terrain that California offers. Some of the SVRAs of Southern California provide large desert areas and trails to ride. (Photo Courtesy Pan photo/Shutterstock.com)

Southern Utah has a lot of wide-open spaces to explore with some trails that go on for miles. Some of these trails are historic, and most are very remote. The Native American presence is heavy here with ancient art and dwellings being easy to find. Off-road trails lead to the Green River, Colorado River, and Lake Powell. There are groups that drive across Southern Utah on a "Traverse" route, taking dirt roads and trails as much as possible. The Rimrocker Trail is a 160-mile off-road trip that starts in Montrose, Colorado, and ends in Moab, Utah. The Burr Trail is an old cattle trail designed to move cattle between their summer and winter ranges. (Photo Courtesy Wirestock Creators/Shutterstock.com)

Colorado is known for its high-elevation hiking, biking, and skiing. However, there are plenty of off-road trails too. Many established trails can be found between Ouray and Silverton. The Buena Vista trails are also popular. There are even dirt roads leading to old ghost towns and mines. About 99 percent of off-road trails in Colorado are on public land. (Photo Courtesy Laurens Hoddenbagh/Shutterstock.com)

The hundreds of trails around Moab, Utah, are a big draw. There are trails within the Arches and Canyonlands National Parks nearby. This is a huge destination for off-road enthusiasts of all kinds. The coarse red rock provides incredible traction, allowing you to drive up and down some very steep hills. Other areas are sandy, and there are easy scenic trails that allow you to see for many miles without any evidence of man. There are also some very difficult trails. It is wise to ask local 4WD shops or guides about the trails in which you are interested. Do not rely on internet experts for the latest information.

Southern Utah also has some very remote trails that are incredible but less famous. The Hole in the Rock Trail is historic and challenging. The Maze District of Canyonlands National Park is probably the most remote trail system in the United States. You must be self-reliant and prepared to travel there.

Utah also has Sand Hollow State Park. For longer excursions on dirt roads, check out the Burr Trail and the Rimrocker Trail. Capital Reef National Park has dirt roads through the Cathedral Valley. In addition, the Valley of the Gods is another scenic off-road destination.

Colorado has an amazing number of 4WD trails. Look up the "Stay the Trail" website for ideas. Some are easy scenic county dirt roads, while others are insane. Consider Southwest Colorado with the Alpine Loop Trail and many other local trails. Some have preserved ghost towns.

When looking for longer off-pavement drives, do some research about the Backcountry Discovery Routes. Although they are planned for motorcyclists, the routes are open to full-size 4WD vehicles

CHAPTER 3

If you have the time and enjoy traveling, camping, and cooking, consider the Backcountry Discovery Routes and the Trans-America Trail (TAT). These routes can keep you busy for several days. They typically run for several hundred miles, but they can be broken up into segments. They can also connect from state to state and up to 2,000 miles. (Photo Courtesy toseeg/Shutterstock.com)

The Pacific Northwest has heavily forested trails and a few drivable beaches. There are at least two dozen trails within Washington and Oregon on state and federal land. (Photo Courtesy Nature's Charm/Shutterstock.com)

too. These longer trips are sometimes called "traverses," and they can go from one side of a state to the other. Georgia, Utah, and several other states have these routes. Another option is to look up the Trans-America Trail (TAT).

The Pacific Northwest gets a lot of rain, and the forests are very lush. The soil is dark and loamy. Wildfires affect this region, so it's not unusual to find a burned area. Old logging roads and trails are common but are often on private land and require permission to use. Trespassing can get you into a lot of trouble. However, there are quite a few public trails too, and some of the beaches are open to vehicle travel.

Arizona has dozens of beautiful trails—some are among the red-rock beauty of Sedona. Others have historic sites from the Old West and much older Native American art. There are also some very difficult trails from which to choose if you prefer.

Back East

In the East, there are relatively few public trails. Check the national forests for dirt roads and trails that allow full-sized licensed vehicles. Be aware that our federal land management agencies, the US Forest Service (USFS) and Bureau of Land Management (BLM), often offer separate trails for ATV/UTV/motorcycle riders.

In West Virginia, consider the Hatfield-McCoy Trails. Kentucky has the 150-mile Daniel Boone Backcountry Byway near Slade. In Florida, the Big Cypress National Preserve near the Everglades and the Ocala National Forest has 81 miles of unpaved roads.

Georgia only has one small trail system for full-size 4WD vehicles,

ADVENTURES

Arizona and New Mexico have scenic dirt roads and trails that were used in the Old West. However, they also have some very challenging rock crawling trails that will test anyone's driving skills and vehicle. (Photo Courtesy LHBLLC/Shutterstock.com)

while South Carolina has no public trails for 4WD vehicles at all. North Carolina has four trail systems that allow full-size, street-legal 4WD trucks and SUVs. You get the idea. It's fairly easy to find which trails are available nearby.

Some states, counties, and cities have developed off-road parks to enhance their local economies. The Black Mountain Adventure Area near Harlan, Kentucky, is an example of this. So is the Coalmont OHV Park near Coalmont, Tennessee. There are many other examples.

Of course, private off-highway vehicle (OHV) parks exist where public trails are scarce. Eastern parks include Windrock Park near Knoxville, Tennessee (73,000 acres), and the Southern Missouri Off-Road Ranch near Springfield, Missouri. In the coal-producing area of Pennsylvania, there are the Rausch Creek and Anthracite Outdoor Adventure areas.

The eastern United States was the first part to be settled. The early citizens were trying to survive by building towns and farms. They weren't worried about keeping land available for public parks. The majority of Americans live in the eastern United States, so housing and businesses have taken over many large tracts of open land. There are some state and federal parks in the East that allow 4WD vehicles, but they are scarce. (Photo Courtesy Gorlov-KV/Shutterstock.com)

A bit of online research will help you find the public trails in each state. Knowing who manages the trails will help in finding when the trails are open or closed and current conditions. It's still a good idea to run these trails with someone who already knows them—at least for the first few times. (Photo Courtesy OPOLJA/Shutterstock.com)

THE ULTIMATE OFF-ROAD DRIVER'S GUIDE

CHAPTER 3

In places where there are few public trails, private OHV parks can sometimes be found. These private parks often cater to UTVs and motorcycles because there are so many of these machines in use. They tend to be small because land is scarce and there is high cost to buying and maintaining the land. There are exceptions, but most trails in private parks tend to be short and range from moderate to high difficulty. (Photo Courtesy Windrock Park)

Getting to the Trail

It's a common experience to meet people who are exploring far from home. They may already know the trails in their area and want to see different scenery and terrain. For some folks, seeing huge rolling sand dunes is amazing, while for others, seeing the lush, green forests and waterfalls is magical.

Friends and families sometimes caravan together and camp in RVs or rent condos in popular off-roading areas. It can be fun to share the experiences with people you know and trust. In addition, you'll have witnesses for the campfire stories later.

One decision to make is whether to fly out to a popular off-roading area and rent a 4WD SUV or to pull your own vehicle out and back. There are pros and cons to every option. Time and cost need to be considered.

Flying and renting a 4WD eliminates the long drive to and from the destination. However, you must verify that the 4WD vehicle can actually be picked up at the airport. A rental car may actually be needed to get to the town that has a rental 4WD. However, saving the paid time off (PTO) from work has value, and there's no need for a truck/RV and trailer to pull your 4WD out and back. Consider the amount of fuel that it takes to tow and the additional nights in a motel or campground. Lastly, be realistic about the condition of your 4WD. Rental 4WDs are typically new and reliable.

If time is not an issue and sightseeing while crossing the country is the goal, then by all means tow your own 4WD. Check with motels and campgrounds to verify that they have parking for a 40- to 60-foot rig. If you don't own a vehicle built for towing,

Flat towing requires the least amount of equipment, but it also requires the most caution. The 4WD vehicle needs to be suitable for flat towing. It needs to have a manually operated transfer case that can be put in neutral. A manual transmission needs to be in first gear, and an automatic transmission needs to be in park. The steering wheel needs to be unlocked. A portable brake system needs to be added for safety. The front tires, axle shafts, and driveshafts will spin as it is towed along. (Photo Courtesy Karin Hildebrand Lau/Shutterstock.com)

rent a pickup truck from U-Haul that is rated to tow up to 6,000 pounds. You can rent a trailer there too. Their trailers are fairly short and heavy, so verify that your 4WD will fit and meet the weight limits.

If you tow with a motor home, verify its towing capacity. Diesel-powered RVs can typically tow more than gas-powered RVs. Finally, consider the route. If you are towing the maximum load, driving steep mountain highways will redefine your idea of slow. You may also find religion as you begin to smell the brakes when you are going down the other side.

Flat Towing

Whether towing with a truck or an RV, there are several towing options. The least expensive is flat towing. Flat towing means that all four tires are on the ground being pulled along by a tow vehicle. A vehicle can be flat towed if it has four-wheel drive and a manual transfer case that can be placed in neutral. Jeep Wranglers are often flat towed. Toyota specifically states that its vehicles with an automatic transmission cannot be flat towed.

When flat towing, there is more to consider than bolting a tow bar to the front bumper. The tow vehicle needs a trailer hitch and wiring harness to make the towed (toad) vehicle's taillights and brake lights work. There are aftermarket braking systems that apply the towed 4WD vehicle's brakes. Otherwise, the tow vehicle will need to be able to stop itself and the towed 4WD. Chances are good that the tow vehicle wasn't engineered to stop that much weight.

Disconnect the battery and turn the ignition key so that the steering wheel is unlocked. This allows the 4WD vehicle to follow the towing vehicle around corners.

In general, put the transfer case in neutral. Then, put a vehicle with a manual transmission in first gear or a vehicle with an automatic transmission in park. This prevents the transmission from spinning but allows the transfer case to turn.

Even with this setup, the rear tires will spin the rear driveshaft, which in turn, spins the transfer case. Be sure that the transfer case will receive the lubrication that it needs to survive. If not, the rear driveshaft will probably need to be removed to stop the transfer case from spinning.

CHAPTER 3

For trailering, simply drive onto the trailer and strap the 4WD vehicle down. A proper car-hauling trailer will have suitable axle bearings, brakes, and tires for the truck or SUV's weight. The downside with trailers is usually their year-round storage and during parking on trips due to their length. (Photo Courtesy Ogletree Photography/Shutterstock.com)

Learn about your 4WD vehicle's suitability before attempting to flat tow it.

Tow Dolly

The next method of towing is using a tow dolly. They are expensive and can cost as much as a trailer. These can be rented. Their primary advantage is that they are small and don't take up much space at a campground or at home. However, they still leave the rear tires on the ground.

To use one, attach the dolly to the trailer hitch and then basically drive the front tires up onto a pair of metal ramps on wheels. Then, strap the front tires down. Be sure that the tire nets or straps are big enough to get over the off-road tires. Most tow dollies are used for towing small cars. The better-quality tow dollies do have electric or surge brakes. Electric brakes require a brake controller in the towing vehicle.

Trailering

Another option is to put the 4WD vehicle on a trailer and connect it to the truck or RV. This requires no changes to the 4WD truck or SUV. In addition, if the 4WD breaks a drivetrain part, simply load it onto the trailer and take it where needed.

Many drivers will say that it's easier to pull a trailer than a dolly or flat-towed vehicle. You can't back up when flat towing and dollies can sway or whip side to side.

Trailers have their own tires, brakes, and lights. They are sturdy and rated for towing a heavy 4WD. Of course, there is additional expense to maintain the bearings, tires, and brakes. Parking trailers can also be a challenge in some places due to their length.

Aluminum trailers are lighter but more expensive. Lighter trailers allow for towing a heavier 4WD and not exceeding the trailer's axle rating. The less weight that you tow, the better it is for the tow vehicle, fuel mileage, brakes, etc.

Steel trailers with a wooden deck can be a good compromise on weight and cost. However, the wood will need to be protected with deck stain and replaced every few years.

Nearly all car-hauling trailers are built with a pair of 3,500-pound-capacity axles. This is usually adequate, but add the weight of your 4WD vehicle and the trailer to be sure. Ordering 5,000- or 7,000-pound axles can be a good investment. They come with larger bearings, brakes, and tires. They also run cooler and last longer.

America is blessed with a lot of land, and in some places, there are still dirt roads and trails that we can explore and enjoy. Go have fun!

CHAPTER 4

ORGANIZING A TRAIL RIDE

At some point, you may organize a trail ride. This can be a lot of work, but it is usually very rewarding, especially if it goes well. There's a saying that "If you're not the lead dog, the view never changes."

You and your tail gunner should reset your tripometers at the trailhead and track the time and mileage between scenic locations and wide spots for rest breaks and lunch. Intersections and exits to paved roads need to be noted as well. Take note of the trail's difficulty and obstacles.

As with many things in life, the success of the trip depends on good planning and communication. A bit of luck always helps. This is primarily because no one can control the weather.

Organizing a trail ride for a group of people has similarities to planning your own ride, but there is more to consider. Picking a date is a good start. Consider whether the proposed date conflicts with a holiday or other regional 4WD event. Do people prefer a Saturday or a Sunday? If you are raising a family, it's pretty common to have your Saturday filled with children's activities; a Sunday may actually work better.

If this will be a one-day trip, consider that people need enough time to drive to your meeting place in the morning and enough time to drive home afterward. How far are people typically willing to drive? One hour is a good start. Don't be afraid to get opinions from people who show interest in your ride. You can ask at a club meeting or in an online poll. This will help you decide on which trails to focus.

Next, consider the audience and the difficulty of the trail. Is this supposed to be an easy, moderate, or hard trail ride? This will help narrow the trail selection. When in doubt, pick a trail that's a little easier rather than a bit harder. Trail ratings are subjective. One person's opinion about what is moderate may differ from another's.

Have a backup trail in mind in case the weather changes close to the trail ride date. Know the trail options well enough to know whether the difficulty will change with rain or snow. Traction on rocky trails usually doesn't change radically after some rain. Sand tends to absorb the rain and drain the water away. However, loamy soil and clay can be muddy and slick after rain or snow.

Also, consider some what-ifs. What if we are delayed on the trail due to a breakdown. Is there an intersection that allows us to return to pavement sooner? What if we get to the end of the trail early? Is there something else we can do to fill some time? If not, go find ice cream or a scenic spot to gather.

Once a trail or two have been selected that meets the group's needs, go pre-run them. Take your tail gunner (the last driver in the trail ride) and drive the trail.

CHAPTER 4

While a trail may look good on the map, you need to go see it in person. Even if you've ridden it before, go back and run it with a fresh perspective. There's a big difference between following the herd and being out front leading. Take your time and enjoy the day. Exploring and pre-running can be fun. There are no responsibilities or pressures.

The view from the tail gunner's position will fluctuate from seeing every vehicle in line to perhaps just the vehicle in front of them. The tail gunner and lead vehicle stay in communication to prevent missed turns and gaps in the line. The tail gunner can also report if faster traffic has come up behind them. If a vehicle breaks down, the tail gunner will stay behind to help fix it or assist in getting them out. If someone has a medical issue, the tail gunner will escort them to the nearest medical facility. The trail leader and tail gunner need to know where medical assistance is in advance of the trail ride. (Photo Courtesy zeelichsheng/Shutterstock.com)

Tail Gunning

The tail gunner can be a big asset. He or she may actually know the trail better than you but may simply not have the time or want the responsibility of organizing a trail ride. The tail gunner is the person who will be staying behind with anyone who breaks down or needs medical attention. He or she needs to be able to lead or tow that vehicle out to a paved road safely. They also need to know where the nearest repair shop or hospital is located.

On twisting or hilly trails, you may not be able to see all of the vehicles behind you. You'll need to communicate with your tail gunner via radio. The tail gunner is your eyes and ears at the back of the line.

Choosing a good meeting place is important. It needs to be easy to find, be big enough to fit everyone, and provide basic services for drivers as they arrive. At a minimum, it should have a gas station with gas, an air compressor, and a restroom. Ideally, it should be fairly close to the trailhead.

On the scouting trip, be sure that the trail is legally open and that permission has been granted to be there. It's a good idea to take note of landmarks on the trail and how long it takes to get there. You'll also want to take note of turns and distances.

The more vehicles on the trail, the longer it will take to complete the trail ride. It can easily take twice as long to drive a trail when there is a long line of folks behind you.

Look for wide places along the trail to pull over and let people have a restroom break. This spot needs to have cover for privacy. You'll also want to find a scenic spot for lunch. You may even want to take some pictures to promote your ride.

If this trail meets most of your criteria, type your notes and use them as directions in the future.

Advertising

Next, start communicating with prospective drivers about what to expect: the date, meeting time, departure time, type of radio being used, estimate of how long the ride should last, etc. Insert a few pictures as a tease but not too many. People want to see new things and be surprised.

Create a sign-up list to know how many vehicles plan on coming and how they are equipped. It is important to know the driver's name, vehicle type, number of passengers and pets, phone number, and email address.

Set a limit on the group size. It's not unusual for rides organized on forums to have a large turnout. It's also fairly typical that about 25 to 30 percent of people will drop out or not show up.

Most experienced trail leaders say that the limit for an easy trail ride should be somewhere around 12 to 15 vehicles. Less-experienced drivers take longer and may need help navigating obstacles. Moderate trail rides should probably be limited to 10 to 12 vehicles. Hard trail rides should have an even smaller group size. Bigger obstacles take longer to get over. These are not hard and fast rules. They are just a place to start. Local trail conditions, weather, and the experience level of the drivers may change these numbers. If the group size is too large, it can negatively impact the experience. You want to avoid having people wait for long periods of time.

If you are leading a trail ride for an organized 4WD club or event, it is common to specify which radio type is required. The two most common choices are CB or GMRS radios. If this trail ride is for random people found on an internet forum, you may want to require family radio service (FRS) radios. They are commonly available and inexpensive. Bring an extra FRS radio or two in case someone forgets. Bringing extra AA batteries can be helpful too.

Selecting a meeting place is important too. It needs to be reasonably close to the trailhead and have enough parking to accommodate everyone. Ideally, this spot should offer a restroom and gas. Some grocery store chains have all of this and a coffee shop.

Time to Go

On the day of the trail ride, you and your tail gunner need to arrive at the meeting place early so that you can take care of your needs before other drivers begin arriving. Don't be surprised to find drivers already there.

As people arrive, greet them and answer any questions. Point out the restrooms, gas pumps, or anything else that may be helpful. Offer a radio check if they want to be sure they can hear you. You may even want to hand each driver a kitchen trash bag so they have something to put their trash in during the day.

CHAPTER 4

Greet people as they arrive. Answer any questions, but allow them enough time to use the restroom, top off with fuel, etc. You can get into the specifics of the trail ride during the driver's meeting.

Briefly mention that you'll be observing the Tread Lightly! principles today. Warn drivers not to make disparaging remarks about the locals. Let people know if they should air down their tires now or at trailhead. Remind people that they should have their lunch, soft drinks, snacks, and a full tank of gas.

Driver's Meeting

Before starting out, have a driver's meeting to set the expectations for the day and get everyone on the same page. Use a brief checklist to cover the various topics during the 5- to 10-minute meeting.

Topics should include safety concerns, such as dehydration, poison ivy, ticks, snakes, stinging insects, and slippery trail conditions. More people get hurt walking around outside of their vehicle than in it. Twisted ankles or sprained wrists are the most common. Children and pets need to be kept close to the trail.

Tell everyone the radio channel that will be used and that they should have their headlights on for safety. Remind drivers to keep radio transmissions short so that the trail leader and tail gunner can call out upcoming turns.

Herding the Cats

Getting from the meeting place to the trailhead can be one of the most difficult parts of the day. Larger groups tend to get split up by other traffic or traffic lights. Keeping everyone together is a challenge. You and your tail gunner need to communicate throughout the drive.

It helps if the trail is near your meeting place. If there is too great of a gap in the line, it may be wise for the vehicles in front to pull over and wait for the vehicles in the back. If your drivers have their headlights on, it can be easier to track who is behind you.

Communication

People appreciate knowing what's going on. If you stop for an obstacle, let people know over the radio. Encourage people to come forward and watch or take pictures. Be aware that they will have to be chased back to their vehicles when it's their turn to drive forward. People like pictures of themselves and their vehicles. It helps document their day and will help them reminisce years later.

Allow enough time for picture taking and maybe a group photo at a scenic spot. You might be surprised how much you'll appreciate these photos later in life and be shocked at how good you looked at the time.

People should be comfortable and feel free to talk on the radio. They should not be afraid to ask for a rest stop when the coffee kicks in. Be approachable and answer questions as well as you can. Don't be deceitful to people; they will eventually find out. Some drivers may want to ask questions after the trail ride. Make sure that they can reach you.

Time Management

A seven-hour day is usually long enough to satisfy people's desire for an off-road experience, especially if there are children or pets along.

A good trail leader will be watching the time throughout the day and adjusting so that the trail ride ends on time. The schedule can be adjusted by speeding up or slowing down on the trail. If necessary, lunch can be shortened to stay on track. Rest stops can be short or long. You will have your landmarks and times from your pre-run notes to get a sense of where you are and how much longer it will take to complete the trail ride.

The driver's meeting will set the tone for the day. Providing brief, concise information about what to expect is critical. People should walk back to their vehicles after the meeting confident that they are ready and know what to expect. Mention the distance to the trailhead, trail conditions, the weather forecast, safety, and the radio channel being used.

ORGANIZING A TRAIL RIDE

Today's Itinerary	
8 a.m.	Arrive at the meeting place
8:20 a.m.	Driver's meeting
8:30 a.m.	Depart to the trail
9 a.m.	Arrive at trail, air down, have secondary driver meeting to discuss the trail and quickly remind people about safety
9:30 a.m.	Depart on the trail ride
Noon	Lunch
4:30 p.m.	End trail ride and drive back to the original meeting place. Air up, refill gas tanks, use restroom, etc.
5 p.m.	Say goodbyes

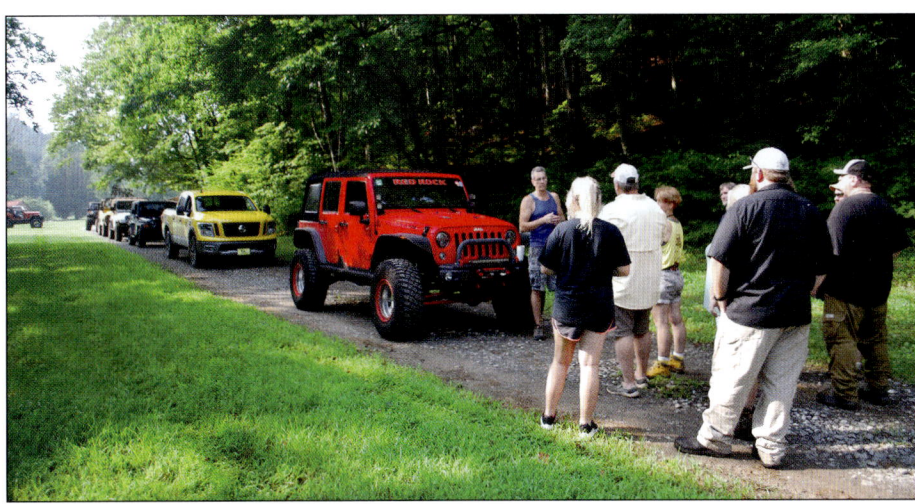

People want to know what's going on, especially if there is a delay. They may not be impatient. They are just curious. Don't make them guess. Their guess can be much worse than what's actually happening. They will also enjoy the day more if they get a bit of information about the local history or the area's scenery. Updates about when the group will stop for a rest break or lunch are also appreciated.

If you are scheduled to be at the lunch spot at noon, but after 2.5 hours of riding, you are not even close, you may decide to have lunch right then and turn around to go back the way you came in. If you reach your lunch spot at 11 a.m., stretch out the afternoon a little by taking longer breaks or driving slower. As the trail leader, you determine the group's speed. They are following you.

One key aspect to remember is that people came out to have fun and enjoy the day, and they will unless you royally screw it up. They understand that there may be unexpected delays or weather changes, but if you explain the situation and tell them how the plan will be adjusted, they usually will be pretty accepting.

From time to time, drivers may approach you wanting a longer or shorter day. Listen to their story and gauge whether the request is urgent or just convenient. If necessary, be firm and remind them that the whole group needs to be satisfied and not just a few individuals. At best, the tail gunner may be able to escort someone to pavement if there is an early exit. However, the driver leaving early runs the risk of getting lost. It's not fair to the other drivers to go past the 5 p.m. end time for the ride. They planned their day around being done at 5 p.m. or so.

Organizing and leading a trail ride can be a lot of work. However, it can be very rewarding when it goes well and people have a good time. Don't be afraid to speak with other experienced trail leaders. With practice, it will get easier.

Organizing and leading trail rides can be a lot of work but very rewarding. At the end of the day, you should have a happy group of people. With experience, it will get easier. Having a good tail gunner can help a lot too. In addition, you'll begin to appreciate all of the other people who did this for your previous trail rides.

THE ULTIMATE OFF-ROAD DRIVER'S GUIDE

CHAPTER 5

DRIVING TECHNIQUES FOR VARIOUS TERRAIN

Paved roads typically offer the best traction. This is how tractor-trailers get the grip needed to move heavy loads. However, once we leave pavement, the traction is usually less. In addition, paved roads are usually fairly level, despite potholes and frost heaves, while off-road trails often have uneven surfaces.

The aspect that makes off-road driving more challenging and fun is changing driving techniques to adapt to less traction and uneven ground.

Improve Grip

The first thing that most drivers do to improve tire grip is to lower tire pressure. Lowering tire pressure allows the tire to conform to uneven surfaces and offers a much bigger footprint.

Lower tire pressure also softens the ride for you and your passengers. At the end of the day, everyone will be more comfortable. So, the question is, "How low do you go?" Well, that depends on the type of wheels, the size of the tires, and the type of tire that is being used.

A rule of thumb is to go down to 20 psi on stock street-oriented tires. These are the tires that you typically get on most new 4WD SUVs. Look for a moderate tire bulge where the tire touches the ground. This pressure will work on most terrain.

More air pressure can always be let out, but remember that the tires need to be reinflated before (or soon after) you reach paved roads. Low tire pressure at highway speeds can overheat the tire's sidewall and cause damage.

If using off-road beadlock wheels, they can go to a much lower tire pressure. However, they also need to be reinflated before driving far on a paved road. Of course, letting air out

Lower tire pressure creates a bigger footprint, which improves grip, especially in slippery conditions. However, it is important to reinflate the tires before driving at highways speeds.

44 THE ULTIMATE OFF-ROAD DRIVER'S GUIDE

DRIVING TECHNIQUES FOR VARIOUS TERRAIN

The ideal tire pressure varies depending on the type of tires, their size, and the terrain. While 20 psi is a good starting point, experiment to find what works best for you. It's easy to let more pressure out, but at some point, you are just lowering your ground clearance. In addition, going too low can damage the wheels if you are driving over rocks.

Having the ability to reinflate tires is important. If the tire pressure is too low or the tire comes off the wheel, it is great to have an air compressor. A tire plug can be used to fix a flat tire and then reinflate the tire. At the end of the trail ride, increase the tire pressure for the drive home.

of the tires is easier than putting it back in. Having a portable air compressor is very helpful.

Having a full-sized spare tire is important too. If a tire bead unseats from the wheel or if the tire is damaged beyond what a tire plug will fix, a full-size spare is needed.

Maximize Articulation

The second most common thing to do is to disconnect the anti-sway bar that nearly all 4WD SUVs and trucks have. The anti-sway bar is designed to reduce body roll on paved roads when going around corners. They work well to keep the vehicle's body level in turns.

Some manufacturers recognize the advantage of disconnecting the anti-sway bar for off-road use. When the anti-sway bar is disconnected, the front axle can move up and down freely and the tires are more likely to stay on the ground. Having both front tires on the ground greatly improves traction.

Engage 4WD

An easy way to double your traction is to engage 4WD. This may seem obvious, but knowing when to engage 4WD and whether you want high or low range will help prevent you from getting stuck.

In general, it is helpful to engage 4WD when leaving paved roads. Using 4WD is a good idea, even when driving on gravel roads. Having the front tires pulling as you go around corners can help prevent skidding.

Nearly all 4WD vehicles have the ability to shift on the fly between 2WD high range and 4WD high range without stopping. This is simply engaging the front axle or disen-

CHAPTER 5

Anti-sway bars are one way that manufacturers limit body roll on the street. However, they limit wheel travel when off-road. They can cause a tire to spin in the air because it can't droop to the ground. Some 4WD vehicles offer a mechanism that allows you to disconnect the anti-sway bar. This helps keep the front tires on the ground over uneven terrain. Traction improves when the tires are on the ground.

gaging it. You are not changing from high-range to low-range gears in the transfer case.

The 4WD high range is best used in slippery conditions when traction is reduced, such as driving on paved roads that are wet from heavy rain or snow. Be sure to shift back into 2WD high range when the road becomes dry to prevent binding and damage.

Some vehicles have automatic 4WD that will shift into 4WD high range when the computer sensors detect tire slippage. Other options include full-time 4WD, which has the front and rear axles engaged all the time but a center differential that prevents binding when turning corners.

It is very important to research and understand how *your* vehicle's 4WD system operates before using it. The owner's manual is a good place to start your research. Then, find a quiet dirt road to practice using the 4WD features *before* they are needed.

Dirt roads, and gravel roads in particular, can cause understeer. This is a condition where you turn the steering wheel in a curve but the truck continues to go straight. Driving on gravel can feel like driving on marbles. Shifting into 4WD high range will engage the front axles and help pull through the curves.

THE ULTIMATE OFF-ROAD DRIVER'S GUIDE

DRIVING TECHNIQUES FOR VARIOUS TERRAIN

Modern 4WD trucks and SUVs are becoming more complex with computerized features. Knowing how to use these features can greatly improve your off-road experience. Owner's manuals can exceed 700 pages, but they are the best source of accurate information. They usually focus on what each button, knob, or menu item does. However, they don't offer insight as to when and where to use these features. Off-road training courses or trial and error teach these lessons.

So why do I need 4WD low range, and when should I use it? The 4WD low range is a second set of gears in the transfer case that triples or quadruples the torque (power) that is applied to the tires.

The first time that you shift into 4WD low range, you will immediately feel the power (torque) and the slow speed that low range provides. Those low-ratio gears allow you to climb or descend steep hills in a slow, controlled manner. They allow you to crawl over rocks or boulders without stalling the engine.

The first time driving in low range, it is amazing. Suddenly, the benefits of 4WD become clear. You can become a social media star with your SUV or truck. Well, maybe . . .

Another benefit of 4WD low

A 2WD car does fine on carefully engineered paved roads but lacks the torque and traction to go very far off-road. Steep hills and slippery dirt roads stop them in their tracks. Having the additional set of low gears in the transfer case made our favorite 4WD vehicles perform much better. The 4WD low range is a game changer and well worth the higher monthly payments if you want to see what lies beyond the paved roads.

CHAPTER 5

Automatic transmissions have greatly improved in recent years. Manufacturers have increased the number of gears, primarily to improve fuel economy. However, a secondary benefit is that there is a greater selection of gears for off-road use. When in 4WD, you can control speed by manually shifting up or down. Manual transmissions are still fun, but the automatics have caught up in performance.

range is that speed can be controlled. It won't feel like you are going too fast and need to ride the brakes. The lower gears will lower top speed to about 25 or 35 mph, depending on how your vehicle is equipped.

A driver with a manual transmission can speed up or slow down by using the transmission shifter and selecting the gear that gives them the speed they want. Modern automatic transmissions can do the same thing and allow you to select the transmission gear without a clutch.

To shift from high-range gears to low-range gears in the transfer case, come to a stop and shift the transmission into neutral. This takes the pressure off the gears in the transfer case and allows you to select the lower gears. Do the same thing to shift back into the high range. It may take a few attempts to shift the high- or low-range gears if there is any pressure on them.

General Techniques

Driving off paved roads requires a few adjustments.

Seat Belt

Wearing a seat belt is just as important off-road as using one on-road. Not only for safety in the case of an accident but also to help keep you comfortably in the seat. As the vehicle bumps and bounces along, you'll be less tired at the end of the day if you don't have to hang on as much.

Seat belts can retract when driving off-road and can become uncomfortable. If getting out of the vehicle when it's not level, it may retract and then not release when you get back in. Using a spring clamp from the hardware store on the seat belt prevents this problem.

Another useful thing to know is that unbuckling a seat belt and getting out of the vehicle on a hill will cause the seat belt to retract and lock. The seat belt will not be able to reconnect until the vehicle is level. This could be dangerous on a steep or off-camber hill. One solution is to use a spring clip to hold the seat belt open while getting out. Then, remove the clamp once you are safely belted in again.

Sitting upright will improve your view and allow you to see the corners of the vehicle. Some factory seats can be raised and lowered with a handle on the side of the driver's seat. This helps too.

Hand Positioning

Use both hands on the steering wheel because the off-road trails wind and twist far more than a typical road. There is a lot more steering

DRIVING TECHNIQUES FOR VARIOUS TERRAIN

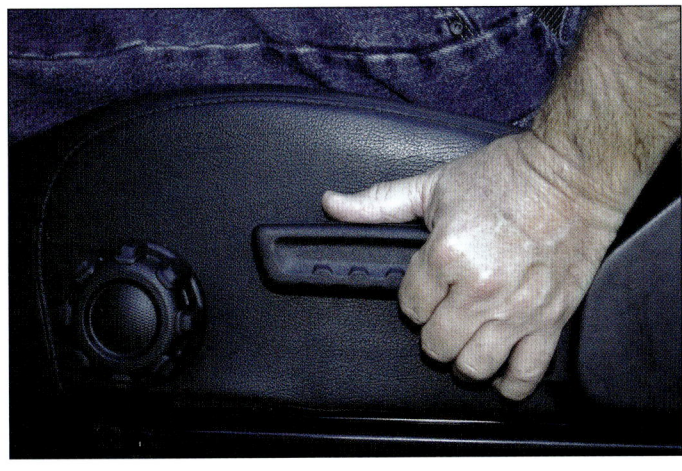

Having the ability to raise the seat helps a driver see ahead. It may be surprising how much more you can see from a higher position.

When driving on the highway, a small movement of the steering wheel will correct the course or allow you to change lanes. However, driving off-road often entails more steering to avoid obstacles. Having both hands on the steering wheel provides greater control and more comfort at the end of the day. Lightly grasping the steering wheel will also help balance your body as you bounce around. Driving over rocks or holes can cause the steering wheel to suddenly kick. That can hurt or even break your thumbs if they are wrapped around the steering wheel spokes. Train yourself to drive with your thumbs on the wheel.

Off-road driving can produce a fair amount of bouncing. When that happens, your right foot can also bounce up and down on the gas pedal. That induces more bouncing. A better way to drive in rough conditions is to plant your heel on the floor and the right side of your foot up against the transmission tunnel. Then, just roll your foot to the left to control the gas pedal. It may look or sound awkward, but you should try it. You may be surprised at how well it works.

that is necessary.

Many people have learned the wisdom of keeping their thumbs on the steering wheel rim instead of wrapped around the spokes. Sudden jerks on the steering wheel are possible when driving over obstacles, and that sudden movement can injure or break a thumb if it's in the way.

Foot Positioning

On rough trails, it's easy to get bouncing along and have the vehicle surge because your right foot is bouncing on the gas pedal. To prevent this, rest your heel on the floor and the right side of your foot against the tunnel. This will steady your foot and help apply the gas smoothly.

Wheel Cheat

One easy mistake to make is to drive too close to trees or other obstacles along the edge of the trail. Starting to turn too soon in a corner will drag the side of the vehicle along the trees or rocks sticking out from the bank. This is called "wheel cheat."

Wheel cheat can be avoided by swinging wide. Make a wider turn to be sure that the whole truck gets by the obstacle, not just the front. The rule of thumb is to drive the front half of the truck or SUV past the obstacle before starting to turn.

Soil Erosion

Erosion is common on trails when water does not drain properly. When a channel erodes down the center of the trail, it is called a rut. Once a rut forms, water will continue to drain downhill in the rut because it now offers the best drainage. Ruts are shallow when they form but become deeper over time. They usually wander back and forth on the trail until

CHAPTER 5

Wheel cheat can happen when turning around obstacles too soon. This is the same thing that happens on the street when a driver turns too tight and a rear tire bounces over a curb. The key is to swing wide enough for the whole vehicle to pass the obstacle.

A rut forms in a trail when there is poor drainage. Water flows down the trail rather than off to the side. Ruts erode over time and can become quite deep. Water typically erodes the softest soil first and then follows that path downhill.

they find a spot where the water can spill over the edge.

The best driving technique for deeper ruts is to straddle them. Place the right tires on one side of the rut and the left side tires on the other. This reduces the chance of getting stuck from falling into the rut.

Eventually, the rut needs to be crossed. Pick a place where the rut is shallow, and cross it at an angle to continue down the trail.

If there is a fallen tree across a trail, determine if it can be driven over without getting stuck. If you are confident that your ground clearance is high enough, then drive across it at an angle. The exact angle is not critical, but generally at a 45-degree angle if possible.

By using this technique, only one tire will be on top of the log at any point in time. The other three tires will be on the ground, providing stability and traction.

Failed Hill Ascent

One thing that scares some people is stalling the vehicle or losing traction while driving up a steep hill. This is called a failed hill ascent. The key here is to apply the brakes, restart the engine if it has stalled, and shift the transmission into reverse.

If you are driving a manual transmission vehicle, let the clutch out. Then, slowly and carefully back down in the original tracks. Use the mirrors or backup camera to guide you back. Stay perpendicular to the hill to avoid a rollover. Ask for help to guide you back down if you need it.

Bump Steer

Another aspect that is unique to off-road driving over uneven terrain

DRIVING TECHNIQUES FOR VARIOUS TERRAIN

Straddling a rut is the best way to navigate this type of obstacle. This will keep the vehicle level and keep all four tires on the ground. If you must cross this form of ditch, cross at the shallowest part. (Photo Courtesy Carl Bush)

is called bump steer. This happens when the uneven ground pushes the steering back and forth. Firmly hold the steering wheel to counteract bump steer and follow the path you want to take. You steer the vehicle; don't let it steer you.

Use the Parking Brake

Get in the habit of setting the parking brake when you stop along the trail. If you make this a habit, you are less likely to watch your vehicle roll down a hill. There is a lot of gravity off-road, and it wants to pull your truck or SUV to the lowest spot possible.

First, pull off to the side of the trail so that others can pass. Then, hold the brakes and shift into neutral. Next, set the parking brake and release the brakes to see if the vehicle moves. If not, shift into park or first gear in a manual transmission.

By doing it this way, the weight of the truck is on the parking brake and not the transmission gears. This will make it easier to leave when you're ready. If the weight of the vehicle is resting on the transmission gears, it can be difficult to shift into drive. Weight on a manual transmission can allow a vehicle to slowly roll forward as the weight overcomes

Crossing a fallen log should be done at an angle so that only one tire is on top of the log at a time. This allows the other three tires to stay on the ground and provide stability and traction. If you get stuck (high-centered) on the log due to low ground clearance, you may be able to back off. Use the mirrors and backup camera if the vehicle is equipped with one.

If backing down a steep hill is needed, use the mirrors or backup camera to keep you perpendicular to the hill and in your own tracks. Veering off to one side or the other can lead to a roll-over and potentially to a long tumble down the hill.

THE ULTIMATE OFF-ROAD DRIVER'S GUIDE

the resistance from the engine's compression.

Be careful when walking around vehicles on the trail. They can shift or move suddenly. Don't walk between two vehicles if at all possible. No one wants to be squished between the bumpers. Walk on the uphill side of a vehicle just in case it moves.

When getting in and out of a truck or SUV, the driver should get in first and hold the brakes before any passengers get in. This way, the driver has control of the vehicle. It can be dangerous to be a passenger if you get in first and the vehicle starts rolling.

The driver should be the last person out of the vehicle. Once everyone else is out, set the parking brake and get out. Follow the first in, last out (FILO) rule.

Mud

Driving on mud can be tricky. Mud typically offers the least traction of any off-road surface. The difficulty of driving in mud depends on the mud's depth and consistency. If a firm dirt road or trail becomes wet due to rain or melting snow, the mud is usually shallow and not too slick. Potholes may simply be filled with dirty water and not mud.

Poorly drained sections of a dirt road or trail can be a nightmare. Having mud tires may help, but even they can become caked in sticky mud.

This is a point where good judgment may cause you to turn around. If you decide to go forward, be prepared to pull the truck from the mud. If there are several muddy tire tracks, pick the straightest and shallowest path. You'll most likely stay in that track from one end of the mud to the other end.

Some mud tires have aggressive sidewalls with sharp lugs that can grab and pull you forward. However, they can also dig holes even faster once forward momentum is lost. When you feel the lack of forward motion, stop!

Snowmelt or heavy rain can create muddy sections of trail due to poor drainage. The consistency of the mud depends on the type of soil and level of wetness. The tire tread design can make a big difference in the success overcoming an obstacle. It's a good idea to consider the what-ifs and the consequences before going forward. It is usually better to get out and look closely at the recovery options. It is also an option to consider turning around.

The responsible thing to do is stay on the dirt road or trail. Do not bypass or go around this muddy section. This will cause even more trail damage and can cause the road or trail to be closed forever. Usually there is no one to come back and fix the trail damage that was caused.

Clay-based soils found in the South and bentonite in the West can be incredibly slick. Even though it is usually not deep, it is so dense and slippery that it can stop anyone in his or her tracks despite using the best off-road driving skills. If you step out of your truck, you may fall down because it is so slick.

The key is to use moderate speed and have steady momentum. Applying too much throttle will only spin the tires faster and may not help. This is one of those trial-and-error skills that will improve with practice.

There are many different consistencies of mud. However, soils with clay are the most slippery. It can be difficult to walk on clay soils and darn near impossible to drive on them. Even those with skills and knowledge may find themselves stuck with spinning tires. Having a friend ahead to pull you out or using a tree nearby as an anchor for your winch is priceless.

DRIVING TECHNIQUES FOR VARIOUS TERRAIN

Once you're stuck, the hard work usually begins. You and your vehicle will probably be a muddy mess. Hopefully there is another vehicle and driver to help pull you forward or back, depending on where there is firm ground. A winch and strong trees will speed up the recovery. Another vehicle and a recovery strap may be a better option. (Photo Courtesy Doidam 10/Shutterstock.com)

The most successful driving technique is to build up a *little* speed before driving into the muddy tracks. If you are driving in a set of muddy tire tracks and traction is lost, try turning the steering wheel back and forth a bit to see if the lugs on the front tire sidewalls will bite and pull you out.

Have the recovery equipment close at hand. It may be a good idea to attach a recovery strap or set up the winch to avoid some of the mess when trying to pull out the truck.

This is another reason to have a good friend with you, especially if they are willing to go first.

Large construction-grade trash bags are great for storing muddy recovery gear once you are back on firm ground. Rubber boots may be a good idea as well.

Lastly, be aware that the mud may stick to the wheels and cause them to be unbalanced once you return to paved roads and accelerate to highway speeds. Tire shops use small lead weights to balance wheels and tires. Imagine what a big clump of mud does to the balancing. Find a self-service car wash and spray the mud off the wheels after a trail ride, if possible. Focus on cleaning the inside of the wheels, steering, and brakes for a safe ride home.

Check the differential fluids when you get home to be sure that they are not contaminated with water. It's also a good idea to add grease to any available grease fittings to squeeze the mud out.

Deep Water

It might be necessary to drive through water to continue down a road or trail. Deep water can cause a number of bad things to happen to a vehicle, and it should be avoided if possible.

The first step when encountering deep water is to know how deep it is. A poor guess can result in the loss of a vehicle or some very expensive repairs. If the water is too deep or the current is too swift, the truck could literally float downstream.

Measure the water depth by wading into the water with a stick or something similar. Find the deepest water in the path. Then, compare that water mark on the stick next to the truck. Most manufacturers advise not going any deeper than the wheel hub.

Deep, flowing water is a serious hazard. It can kill an engine or the sensitive electrical components in a truck. A vehicle can also be swept downstream if the water is deep enough. Flash floods typically occur in the western United States. The saying "Turn around, don't drown" applies here. (Photo Courtesy Monica Garza 73/Shutterstock.com)

Vehicle manufacturers usually tell drivers to go no deeper than the hub (center of the wheel) to maintain the warranty and prevent damage. That may be conservative, but you should venture carefully beyond that depth. (Photo Courtesy Monica Garza 73/Shutterstock.com)

Modern vehicles use a myriad of sensors and computer systems to provide the latest off-road and safety features. None of these components do well when wet. Roadside repairs seldom work when a vehicle gets too wet.

Try to cross from shore to shore using the shortest distance. Be ready to handle a muddy exit on the far shore.

Wading into the stream will also tell you if the bottom is made of mud or slippery rocks. Having the tire pressure lowered and the truck in 4WD will increase traction and help pull you through.

Deep water will rise in the engine bay and over the axles. This can damage the axles, the engine, the transmission, and the transfer case. These components are not waterproof.

The engine, transmission, and transfer case have vent hoses to exchange air as they heat up and cool down. These vents can suck in water. Extending the vent hoses as high as practically possible can help a little, but there are other things that water can ruin too. Modern vehicles use more and more electronics that are very sensitive to being wet. The engine bay may be splash resistant, but it isn't meant to be underwater.

Having a snorkel may raise the air intake for the engine, but it does nothing at all to keep the other drivetrain components dry.

The best technique when driving through water is to keep a slow but steady momentum to keep moving forward. A small bow wave below the front bumper may help form a bubble under the engine. Driving too fast will only cause more splashing under the hood.

Sand

Driving on sand can be fun, but it requires finesse to be successful. There are many varieties of sand, and they are usually defined by the coarseness. Some sand has large, rough grains, while other sand may be a fine powder. Flowing water creates sand, and it is actually made of finely ground rocks and shells.

Damp sand compresses better than dry sand and offers better traction. Dry sand is usually aerated (windblown) and soft. It will also compress when it is driven on, but it will create more drag on the tires.

 **Never Shift a Manual Transmission Midstream**

If a manual transmission is shifted midstream, water will get between the clutch plate and pressure plate and cause the clutch to slip. This will stop you in your tracks. Shift into the correct gear before entering the water. If the engine stalls, leave the clutch engaged and pull the vehicle out with a winch or a recovery strap. ∎

The moisture level in sand will change its color. Dark sand has more moisture and is usually firmer. Lighter sand is drier and can be softer. There are a million variations, but the coarseness of the sand and the moisture level will affect the driving experience. (Photo Courtesy Hundley Photography/Shutterstock.com)

Finding the right speed to drive on sand can be one of the greatest challenges and biggest rewards. That speed varies, depending on the sand's consistency. Seat time and experience are the best teachers. When you get it right, you will feel it. (Photo Courtesy Jimack/Shutterstock.com)

Wet Sand

When driving along a beach, the damp sand along the water's edge is usually firm, but the dry sand above the high tide line is usually soft. This doesn't mean to drive in the water along the ocean's edge at the beach. The swimmers hate that, and the salt water will cause corrosion under the vehicle.

If you are planning to drive on a beach, lower the tire pressure, shift into low range, and enter the sand with a slow and steady momentum. This should carry you through the soft, dry sand and down to the wetter sand along the high-tide line. Better traction should be found there.

With experience, observing the color will help you determine damp versus dry sand. Damp sand is typically darker, and dry sand is often lighter in color.

If you need to stop, try to find darker, firmer sand. This may allow you to start again without spinning the tires. When exiting the beach, use the same technique. Know that as you go higher on the beach, the sand will be dryer and softer. Maintain a steady momentum until you reach the road. Then, reinflate the tires to street pressure to prevent tire damage.

One of the most essential lessons to learn is to start, stop, and turn gently. Aggressive driving can cause the tires to spin or dig into the sand.

Stuck in Sand

Getting stuck in sand can involve a lot of work to dig out and get started again. Having recovery gear is important. A shovel, recovery strap, and shackle (or traction boards) can mean the difference between driving home and walking home.

On beaches, your speed may be regulated by the state for the safety of pedestrians and other vehicles. If you are allowed, drive at your own pace. Find a speed where the vehicle is not going too slow and plowing through the sand and where it's not going too fast with spinning tires and fishtailing.

It's hard to describe, but when you find the right speed, you can feel everything get easier. The engine isn't struggling, the steering is light, and you're just flowing along.

The United States has sand in some unexpected places. Silver Lake State Park in Michigan has awesome sand dunes and is a 4WD playground. The Sand Hollow State Park in southwest Utah is a playground well. The Great Sand Dunes National Preserve in Colorado has the tallest dunes in the United States. Oregon and California have state and federal parks with sand dunes that allow off-road driving in a few places.

Sand Dunes

Driving on sand dunes is different than along a beach. Sand dunes are higher, steeper, and have drier sand than a beach. Dryer sand and steeper dunes require more power and speed to avoid getting stuck. Be aware that

CHAPTER 5

The United States has sand in some of the most unusual places, including Michigan and Colorado. Naturally, it can also be found on the coasts. Access to the beaches and dunes can be restricted, but there are places where driving on sand is allowed. One good thing is that any tracks will be blown away or washed away fairly quickly, leaving no trace that you were there. (Photo Courtesy JoMarie Fecci)

engines and automatic transmissions can overheat when pushing through soft sand in the dunes.

Driving on dunes is more challenging. If you plan on cresting the dune and going down the other side, have enough speed to reach the crest and get over the peak but not so much speed that you go airborne. Most drivers will get a good momentum going and then let off the throttle near the top to prevent flight.

Obviously, you need to know what's on the other side of the dune that you just climbed. A technique to learn is to turn at the dune's crest and drive along the ridge while looking down the far side for other vehicles.

Safety flags are often used to help drivers see each other in this situation. However, each year, drivers launch vehicles and land on top of someone, causing injuries and damage.

Marketing folks like to publish pictures of their vehicles carving a large arc on the side of a sand bowl. It looks awesome and can be fun. However, like most things in life, it requires practice.

Gather speed by going round and round the bowl and then either go out the top or drop back down to the bottom. If you try this and go too slow, there is a risk of rolling over and over down to the bottom. To prevent that, turn downhill and accelerate if the vehicle feels like it is getting tippy.

Sand Hole

One unexpected surprise can be the presence of a witch's hole. This occurs when swirling sand forms a

Driving on steep sand dunes is a lot of fun, but it's important to know where other people and vehicles are located around you. (Photo Courtesy JoMarie Fecci)

Momentum is your friend on sand. Use a nice steady motion with wide arcs. Gentle starts, stops, and turns work the best. (Photo Courtesy JoMarie Fecci)

Dangers to look for among the dunes include this "witch's hole," which was caused by swirling winds. Enjoy the ride but pay attention to where you go. (Photo Courtesy JoMarie Fecci)

hole or depression near the base of a dune. They can be hard to see and dangerous.

Running sand dunes can be endless fun. The dunes are always moving and changing shape. There are many lessons to learn, so it may be a good idea to start by going with someone more experienced than you are. There is no substitute for hands-on practice.

Snow

Many people drive in snow as a routine part of their daily commute. So, we'll skip the challenges and techniques of driving on snowy paved roads. We want to focus on off-road driving.

We'll begin by saying that driving on snow has similarities to driving on sand. All-terrain tires work the best. The siping (tiny grooves) grip the snow and pull you forward. Lowering the tire pressure is essential to get more tire contact on the ground. For stock-size tires, try 20 psi or so and be sure that you have a way to refill the tires before getting back on paved roads. Having a good compressor or a CO_2 tank can be important when you're standing in the cold.

Slow and gentle starts, stops, and turns work best. Quick turns will cause the tires to dig in and kill any momentum. Quick starts or stops can dig holes. Stop immediately if forward motion ends. If the tires aren't moving you forward, they are digging holes.

Anticipate going up hills and try to gently accelerate before getting there to carry your momentum to the top of the hill. When you get to the top, let off the gas and slow down gently going downhill.

Be aware that using differential lockers on an off-camber trail can cause you to slide into a ditch. When the differentials are locked, the tires rotate at the same speed and can act as an auger that is pulling you to the low spot. If you are in a ditch, the lockers may help you drive forward and get back on the trail.

If you get stuck, gently rocking a vehicle back and forth can compress the snow enough to create traction, but spinning the tires melts snow into ice. Rocking a vehicle is worth trying and can work, but be patient and gentle.

Tire chains can go a long way to prevent getting stuck. Speak with local 4WD enthusiasts to see what their experience has been with different style chains and brands. Practice mounting the chains and removing them before they are really needed in the snow. It's a lot easier to learn at home than on the trail.

Given the rocks and tree limbs that might be encountered when

Traction can be scarce in snow. There is a fine line between moving forward and spinning the tires. Gentle acceleration is wise. So are gentle turns and stops. Having a snow shovel and recovery gear can save the day and get you home comfortably. (Photo Courtesy Alenna/ Shutterstock.com)

Snow chains won't make you invincible, but they'll make a huge difference in traction. Keeping them tight and going slow is important. Sturdy chains will last longer and grip better. Be aware that there can be obstacles under the snow that can't be seen. (Photo Courtesy Olga Aniven/Shutterstock.com)

driving off-road, sturdy chains are a must. To be effective, tire chains need to fit tightly to prevent damage to the wheel wells, steering, brake lines, and suspension. Once installed, chains need to be retightened after driving a short distance. Loose chains can come off or do damage.

Using 4WD low range will keep the speed under control and provide the torque that is required without straining the engine and transmission too much. Ironically, the engine or an automatic transmission can overheat if the strain of pushing through deep snow is too much.

Know that snow covers the ground and all its irregularities. So, rocks and holes can't be seen, but they can be felt while driving. Staying on the trail is important. It is easy to slide off into a ditch.

As expected, having recovery gear in the vehicle is important. Getting stuck is easy; getting out can be harder. Having the usual shovel, recovery strap, shackles, winch gear, and/or traction boards can make the difference between a fun day and a bad campfire story.

Be aware that the time of day and temperature changes can change conditions. In the morning, the temperatures are lower and the snow may be firmer, but as the day progresses and temperatures rise, the snow may become slush. This can be helpful, or it can make conditions muddy. In general, getting an early start is better. The days are short in the winter, and daylight is your friend. Here again, it's wise to go with a small group of experienced drivers when you are learning.

Lastly, be prepared for the weather. Bring extra water and food. Have plenty of gas in the tank. Have extra dry socks, pants, jacket, and a warm hat. You may spend more time outdoors than you think. Knowing the trail conditions and having an area map can prevent unintended overnight adventures.

Rocks

Driving on rocky trails is very different than sand, snow, or mud. Rocks offer more traction, but the traction provided by rocks varies. Generally speaking, rocks in the eastern United States have been worn down over a longer period of time and are smoother than western rocks that are still rough. Sandstone can offer great grip, but wet rocks offer less grip. Using low range is a must to go slow and climb over rocks, as necessary.

Driving in fresh snow can be a magical experience, especially with friends. However, deep snow and tough terrain can make a trail ride longer. In addition, the hours of daylight in the winter are fewer. This is one of those times when it pays to be prepared for the cold and potential breakdowns. (Photo Courtesy Lebedev Maksim/Shutterstock.com)

DRIVING TECHNIQUES FOR VARIOUS TERRAIN

Rocks are unforgiving. When driven over slowly, they may bump or scrape a little. However, if driven over too fast, they can damage a vehicle. Speed thrills, but speed kills. My goal is to avoid being in a YouTube video that goes viral.

At first, you may attempt to drive over obstacles that are too tall for your ground clearance. This will result in getting "high centered" or stuck. With experience, you can judge obstacles to decide whether you have enough clearance to drive over them. Knowing where your vehicle's low points are helps you pick a safe path.

While sand, mud, and snow generally don't damage a vehicle, rocks can.

There is a saying when playing in the rocks. "Don't hurt the rocks." What is meant by this is that if we don't hit the rocks with our skid plates and body, we won't damage our vehicle either.

Here again, lowering tire pressure is very important. Beadlock wheels can be used at low tire pressures to prevent the tire from coming off the wheel. However, if the tire pressure is too low, there is a risk of damage to the wheel as rocks are hit. Going slow is key. Once again, all-terrain tires provide more tread surface and more grip. The flexible tread can wrap around rocks and pull you forward.

Disconnecting the sway bar will allow the tires to travel up and down more freely. Tires on the ground provide traction; tires spinning in the air don't. Engage the differential lockers if you have them as needed to help you keep moving. Be aware that having the front differential locked greatly increases the turning radius. If you need to make a sharp turn, turn the locker off temporarily. Seat time and practice will improve your skills.

The challenge with driving on rocks is finding a path that offers enough ground clearance to not get high centered. High centering is caused by driving over an obstacle that is too tall for the clearance under the vehicle.

Popular additions to trucks and SUVs that drive on rocky trails are skid plates to protect the drivetrain and rock sliders to protect the rocker panels. Taller suspensions make room for taller tires, which in turn creates more ground clearance. Taller tires may require a whole list of other

THE ULTIMATE OFF-ROAD DRIVER'S GUIDE

CHAPTER 5

Picking a line (safe path) through a series of obstacles can be daunting and look like a maze. However, with practice and a spotter, you will learn how to select the path of least resistance. Think of it as a challenging puzzle.

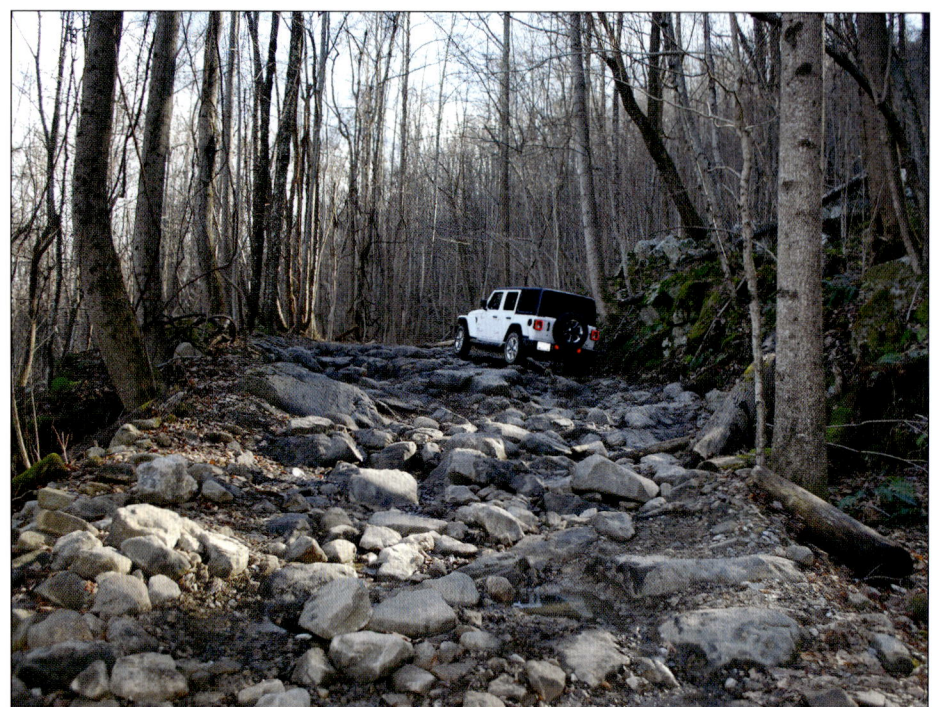

accessories and modifications to compensate for their effects.

Finding the best path through rocky sections of a trail is called "picking a line." When encountering short sections of rocks, try to stop and look for the best path. Memorize the path and some landmarks that provide a clue when to turn left or right.

For longer sections of rock, repeat this process or ask for a spotter. A spotter is a person outside the vehicle who is giving directions through hand signals. A spotter can see the ground and all four tires. This is a great benefit when all you can see is your hood and sky.

Rock crawling can be fun and challenging. Getting unstuck is usually easier than the loss of traction with sand, mud, and snow. Go slow and drive carefully. Keep the vehicle as level as possible to prevent a rollover and to take the path of least resistance to prevent damage to the vehicle. That's not always possible, but it is a worthy goal.

There are times when a slow, steady momentum will keep you rolling over rocks and ledges. If you stop or hesitate at the base of a ledge or rock and lose momentum, you may lose traction. Just try to keep a slow, steady rolling pace. A spotter helping out may tell you to "bump it." This means to give the gas pedal a quick blip to get the front or rear tires up onto the higher ledge or rock.

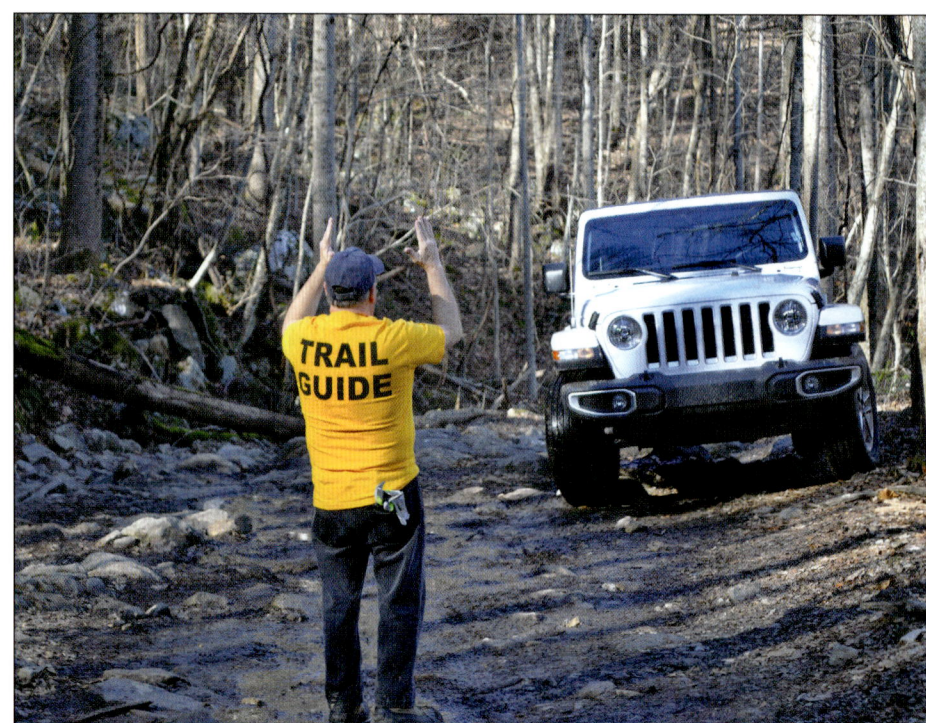

A driver's view is seriously limited when going up steep hills or over difficult obstacles. You can't see the trail itself or the rocks that the tires need to climb. Having a trusted spotter helps immensely. This person can see the trail ahead and where the tires are placed. Hand signals will tell you when to turn and how far. There is no shame in asking for help in these situations. A spotter can prevent a lot of damage or injuries. If you don't have a trusted spotter, let your passenger drive, and you can direct their path.

60   THE ULTIMATE OFF-ROAD DRIVER'S GUIDE

CHAPTER 6

RECOVERY

The most important thing that is needed to prevent getting stuck is knowledge. This is closely followed by hands-on experience. Both of these are available from a 4WD trainer.

The consequences for getting this wrong can be painful and expensive. We all have "helpful" friends on the trail, but remember that it's your deductible for the car insurance and health insurance. It is important to get this right.

Several things can be done to avoid getting stuck. That's the goal. Sometimes it works out, and sometimes it doesn't. Every situation is different. Even your vehicle and driving style can make a difference.

There are two primary reasons that you get stuck.

- Lack of traction
- Lack of ground clearance under the vehicle

When you drive off of paved roads, there is less traction. Soft dirt, gravel, sand, snow, and mud can cause your tires to lose their grip and spin. Spinning tires won't move you forward and can dig holes in the trail. This damages the trail and will cause you to work harder to get unstuck.

Shortly after leaving the pavement, shift into 4WD. Using either high or low range depends on the trail conditions. In addition, let some air out of the tires to provide a bigger footprint. The amount of air that is let out depends on the trail conditions, type of surface, and speed of travel.

When airing down, consider how and where you will air up. Reinflating the tires is important so that you can have a safe drive home.

Disconnect the Sway Bar

If the trail is rough and uneven, you may want to disconnect the

If you can't see an obstacle well or are unsure how to cross it, ask for help. Either your passenger or another driver can get out and look over the situation. They can see where the four tires are and how to drive over the obstacle safely. Keep in mind that only one spotter is needed. Any others who are yelling out ideas should be considered hecklers. In the end, it is your vehicle, and any damage is your responsibility. (Photo Courtesy Brandon VandeCaveye/Shutterstock.com)

THE ULTIMATE OFF-ROAD DRIVER'S GUIDE

CHAPTER 6

As has been discussed, letting some air out of your tires (airing down) will create a larger footprint and better traction. Consider how you'll be able to reinflate the tires before driving on the pavement at highway speeds.

Tires on the ground provide traction. Tires in the air don't. One way to keep the tires on the ground is to disconnect the front anti-sway bar. This can be done manually with basic hand tools or by pressing a button on some 4WD SUVs and trucks with off-road packages. Please remember to reconnect the anti-sway bar before driving on pavement. (Photo Courtesy Ogletree Photography/Shutterstock.com)

Some off-road packages offer either electronic or hydraulic anti-sway bar disconnects. Both systems are operated by a dash-mounted switch that disconnects and reconnects the front anti-sway bar. (Photo Courtesy otomobil/Shutterstock.com)

anti-sway bar. Sway bars are designed to limit body roll (sway) when you go around sharp corners on the road. However, they also limit wheel travel off-road. This causes tires to lift off the ground and spin. Disconnecting a sway bar allows the tires to droop and touch the ground. This will move you forward and can prevent you from getting stuck.

Some 4WD manufacturers sell off-road editions with a button on the dash that disconnects the sway bar.

Left-Foot Braking

With open differentials (unlocked), the torque from the engine is applied to the tire with the least resistance, causing that tire to spin. By applying the brakes gently with your left foot and then slowly adding some throttle with your right foot, you are using the brakes to create resistance to the spinning tire. This transfers some of the torque to the opposite tire that has traction. Sometimes, it can be enough to get moving again. Traction control does this too, so it may be better to let the computers do this for you.

Left-foot braking can also dampen the ride when driving over rough ground and prevent the vehicle from dropping off the backside of a boulder. This technique can also be used to prevent vehicles from rolling backward when stopped on a steep hill, especially when the vehicle is equipped with an automatic transmission. Some modern 4WDs now come with a hill assist feature that prevents rollback.

Lastly, be aware that using the gas and brake pedals at the same time can confuse modern computers and simulate unintended acceleration. This may cause the check engine light to come on.

Traction Control

Many modern vehicles have traction control systems that allow the driver to select the terrain on which he or she is driving. Traction control is a feature that uses a computer, wheel sensors, and the braking system to reduce tire spin. This shifts the engine's torque to another tire that may have better traction.

The engineers recognized that

More and more 4WD vehicles are using selectable traction control to help drivers avoid getting stuck. In the past, traction control was automatic, and the driver had no control over its function. Now, it can be adjusted by the driver when in 4WD. (Photo Courtesy otomobil/Shutterstock.com)

When facing a rough section of trail, select a path that offers the least resistance and keeps the vehicle fairly level. If you can see a path or can follow someone else ahead of you, try it slowly. If you can't see a path or get stuck, have a spotter get out and help.

A person standing outside the vehicle can see the trail far better than anyone in the driver's seat. The spotter can select a path and provide directions with hand signals. It is difficult to hear them if they are yelling, so watch for hand signals.

Applying too much power (torque) to the trail may cause the tires to spin. Shifting up to second gear may allow a gentler start and get the truck moving again. This can be done with manual and some automatic transmissions. (Photo Courtesy maradek/Shutterstock.com)

If the truck or SUV has locking differentials, engage them with the button on the dash. Locking the differentials will apply power (torque) evenly to both tires and may prevent a vehicle from getting stuck. However, if the traction is too poor, locking the differentials will just spin both tires in unison.

some tire spin may be necessary when traveling through sand, snow, or mud, so the computer applies less braking. However, spinning tires on rocks can damage a vehicle, so the computer limits the tire spin allowed on the Rock setting.

Moving the traction control knob to the Sand, Snow, Rocks, or Mud positions, can improve the odds of getting through a rough spot.

Pick a Line

When coming to a section of trail with obstacles, slow down or stop until a path can be found through that section. Ground clearance is usually the main concern. Consider the lowest part of the truck and whether it will pass over the obstacles. Take the path of least resistance and try to keep the truck or SUV as level as possible. This is a skill best taught by a 4WD trainer and one that takes practice to be good.

Spotters are Your Friend

When in doubt, ask for help. A passenger or another driver you trust can get out and look. They will be able to see the line or path you should take. They can also compare that line to the vehicle's ground clearance. This is usually called spotting, and the person helping is known as a spotter.

Spotting may take a few minutes, but it is considerably faster than getting stuck and unstuck. Choose your spotter wisely and trust him or her. The spotter can see the tires and the rocks, ruts, holes, etc. You may only see the hood and sky.

You probably won't be able to hear the spotter, so he or she uses hand signals. Go slow and make small adjustments on the steering

Hand Signals

These are the standard hand signals most spotters use and what they mean.

Spotters use the standard hand signals that everyone understands. If the spotter is the driver's spouse or partner, they may develop their own signals in addition to the standard ones. This hand signal means that the driver should turn left (from the spotter's point of view), which is the direction in which the spotter is pointing.

This hand signal means to turn right (from the spotter's point of view). Turn in the direction in which the spotter is pointing.

This hand signal means to stop immediately but safely.

This hand signal means to come forward slowly.

This hand signal means to back up slowly.

CHAPTER 6

If the truck or SUV needs to be lifted a small amount to create more ground clearance, try stacking rocks in front or behind the tires, depending on whether you want to go forward or back. Then, gently apply gas to climb up on the rocks that were stacked. If that works, the vehicle should be free of the obstacle and the driver needs to pick a better path. Be sure to wear gloves to protect your hands and scatter the rocks when you're done.

Lock 'Em if You Got 'Em

There may be instances where use of locking differentials is helpful. Lockers apply the engine's torque evenly to the left and right tires. This can keep you moving if one of the tires slips. Not everyone has them, but if you do, they can be turned on as needed. Typically, it is best to turn on the rear locker first. If conditions are very sandy, muddy, or rocky, turn on the front *and* rear lockers temporarily.

When using the front locker, it may be more difficult to steer and your turns may be much wider. A locked front axle wants to go straight. Turn off the front locker after the rough trail section is cleared.

Using lockers can also create a bind in the driveline, so it's a good idea to turn them off once the obstacle has been passed. This releases the stress on the truck's parts.

wheel. Be prepared to stop quickly if necessary.

The spotter needs to stand in a place where he or she can make eye contact with the driver. That may mean needing to squat down or finding higher ground. The spotter needs to stop periodically and look behind him or her to verify that the vehicle is being led on the correct path. Ideally, the spotter stands where the driver wants to go. This saves a lot of hand signaling. Simply drive toward the spotter.

Spinning Tires Won't Get You Home

Overpowering the available traction will spin the tires. You can upshift the transmission to a higher gear to apply less torque. Shifting a manual or automatic transmission to second or even third gear allows a gentler start and may allow the vehicle to drive off.

When you get stuck, get out to determine why. If you are hip deep in smelly mud, the reason will be obvious without having to leave the seat. However, if you are high-centered, it is best to see what you're stuck on and to determine how to get off the obstacle. Sometimes, the differential is a sticking point because it is often the lowest point underneath the vehicle. In other cases, a skid plate in the center of your vehicle may be the sticking point.

RECOVERY

If lifting the truck is needed and there are no rocks nearby, a jack can be used. A Hi-Lift-style jack and Lift-Mate accessory can lift one tire at a time off the ground. Once that tire is lifted, fill in under it with debris or makeshift blocks. Two or more tires may need to be lifted to get off the obstacle.

When using a recovery strap or rope, be sure that they are strong enough for your purposes. Proper recovery gear will have a label showing the working load limit (WLL) and minimum breaking strength (MBS) ratings.

"Mechanical sympathy" is a term that describes being gentle with a truck's drivetrain when possible. It reduces the amount of repairs needed and improves the chances of driving home safely after the trail ride.

How to Get Unstuck

Despite your best efforts, you will get stuck. Sooner or later, it happens to everyone. Sometimes it's easy to get unstuck, and other times it makes a great story for the campfire later.

So, let's figure out what went wrong and how to fix it. As mentioned earlier, getting stuck is usually due to a lack of traction or ground clearance. Often, it is possible to determine what happened before even getting out of the truck. Are the tires howling as they search for grip or was there a horrible screeching noise while driving over the rocks?

Use recovery straps with caution. Often, only a gentle pull is needed. The straps have nylon in them that stretches and gives an elastic pull. The recoil can be strong, so only use strong frame-mounted tow points. More than one bumper has been pulled off by a recovery strap that wasn't securely attached.

Get Out and Look

The key to the safe recovery of a stuck vehicle is to remain calm and think clearly. Assess exactly why you're stuck and determine the best method to get unstuck. Sometimes the simplest method works best.

It may sound crazy, but if you are lightly stuck on an obstacle, the first thing to try is backing up. It's amazing how often this works. With an automatic transmission, shift into reverse and gently apply the gas. Have your left foot hovering over the brake pedal in case you need to stop quickly.

With a manual transmission, shift into reverse and ease the clutch out. Be prepared to push it back in quickly. Go back a few feet to where the truck wasn't stuck. Then, reconsider your options.

Let's Get High(er)

If an obstacle has been driven over that is taller than the vehicle's ground clearance, determine what's actually hitting. Consider whether it's easier to go forward or backward.

One easy technique to gain ground clearance is to put on sturdy gloves and stack nearby rocks in front of or behind the tires. The rocks will form a ramp to lift the vehicle off the obstacle as it drives forward or backward.

Once you're done, scatter the rocks so that the next driver can enjoy the natural challenges that the trail provides.

A recovery strap or a rope with looped ends that are attached to a tow point are safe options.

Receiver hitches are securely bolted to the vehicle's frame and qualify as a frame-mounted tow point. Slide the recovery strap or rope's looped end into the 2-inch receiver and slide a hitch pin through the side holes. A hitch clip will keep things in place. This will securely attach the strap or rope.

A similar technique is to use a jack to lift each tire up a little and stick rocks or other debris under the tire. This requires more effort. The factory jack, a floor jack, a bottle jack, or a Hi-Lift-style jack can be used. Once again, wear sturdy gloves to protect your hands.

Using a Hi-Lift jack requires an accessory called a Lift-Mate that has a pair of hooks that fit through the wheel's spokes. This lifts just one wheel and tire, not the whole vehicle. It is also possible to buy or make a wide, sturdy base for under the jack to be sure that it doesn't sink.

"Spinning Wheels Got to Go Round"

If a vehicle is stuck due to a lack of traction, consider using other techniques and equipment.

One of the most basic pieces of recovery gear is a recovery strap or kinetic-energy recovery rope (KERR). Check the strength rating before buying one to be sure it's strong enough for your vehicle. Vehicle recovery gear will have a label that states the working load limit (WLL) and minimum breaking strength (MBS). A better rating method is the minimum tensile strength (MTS).

Recovery straps and ropes have nylon in them that allow them to stretch up to 30 percent. This means that the typical strap or rope can stretch 4 to 6 feet. Once stretched, it wants to recoil. This bungee effect will often pull out the stuck vehicle.

Be sure that the recovery strap or KERR rope has looped ends. There are some tow straps available with metal hooks on each end. They are not safe for recovery use on the trail. The metal hooks can break under load and become shrapnel.

Consider the weight of the vehicle and the resistance of the mud, snow, or sand in which you are stuck. For example, the weight of an average SUV or midsize pickup is around 5,000 to 6,000 pounds when loaded.

Now, add the resistance, often called the mire resistance. If the vehicle is lightly stuck, add 75 percent of its weight. If it's stuck to the doors, add 150 percent of the vehicle's weight. Add more weight if pulling the stuck vehicle uphill.

So, if the truck weighs 6,000 pounds and it's moderately stuck on level ground, add another 4,500 pounds. That will require a recovery strap or rope with a WLL of at least 10,500 pounds.

It is a mistake to buy a recovery strap or rope that is way overrated for what is needed. That's because the truck won't have enough weight to properly stretch it. It is the stretch and recoil that makes it work. A 3/4-inch or 1-inch recovery rope should effectively pull out a loaded SUV or midsize pickup truck from most situations. A 2-inch-wide recovery strap will also do the job. These straps and ropes are available in different lengths. A 30-foot strap is a good length for general use.

Attaching a recovery strap or rope is easily done if both vehicles have frame-mounted tow hooks. Simply slide the looped end over the tow hook and you are ready to go. However, some vehicles don't come equipped with proper tow hooks.

Bow and soft shackles can attach a recovery strap or a rope to a tow point. Both are rated for this type of work. Just make sure that there are no sharp edges that might cut or fray a soft shackle.

Bow shackles come from the rigging industry and are tough. Just be sure to thread the pin in finger tight and then back up the pin a quarter turn to prevent it from binding when pressure is applied. Many people have cursed when they found that the pin was stuck.

It's easy to lose the bow shackle pin when doing recovery. The vehicle may be on uneven ground, the gear may be slippery, and you may be working while wearing gloves. Inserting the pin with the threads down reduces the chance of dropping it.

CHAPTER 6

Soft shackles are lighter, stronger, and a one-piece design. Threading the ball through the loop may be a little awkward, especially with gloves on. Be sure nothing can cut or fray them when in use.

Check to see if factory tow hooks are available at the local dealership. They were sometimes offered as a factory option. If available, they will bolt on and be rated for the vehicle's weight.

If the truck has a frame-mounted 2-inch or larger trailer hitch, it will work. Instead, remove the drawbar and slide the loop inside the receiver. Then, reinsert the hitch pin. Now, the recovery strap or rope is securely attached.

Never attach a recovery strap or rope to a trailer ball. The ball will snap off and recoil through the grille or windshield of the stuck vehicle. There are plenty of online videos showing the results.

A lot of damage can be done if a recovery strap or rope is connected to any steering, suspension, or brake parts. Connect them to the frame or a sturdy bumper that's designed for this much force.

If one or both of the vehicles have steel frame-mounted bumpers with holes or brackets designated for recovery, they can be used. However, a shackle is needed to attach the recovery strap or rope to this bumper.

Don't Screw Up

Screw pin bow shackles have been in use in the rigging industry for many decades. The bow shape is used because it accommodates the looped ends of recovery or tree-saver straps and ropes. They are very durable.

Bow shackles also need to be rated for the load being pulled. The same concerns apply regarding the WLL.

The WLL is embossed on the side of the shackle. Typically it is best to use a 3/4-inch shackle with a WLL of 4¾ tons (9,500 pounds).

The breaking strength of these shackles is tested to six times the working load limit. So, a WLL of 4.75 tons typically breaks at about 28 tons during a destructive test. The screw pin will usually be 7/8 inch for this size of shackle, and you'll want to be sure that the pin will fit through the hole on the bumper.

When screwing the pin into the shackle, screw it in finger tight. Then, back it off a quarter turn. If this key step is forgotten, the screw pin may bind up during the pull and it will be a struggle to get it out. Do not lubricate the screw pin threads.

One last piece of advice. "Screw down, don't screw up." It is easy to drop or lose the screw pin when using bow shackles, especially if gloves are being worn. Screwing the pin down into the shackle makes you less likely to drop it.

Soft shackles are a more recent arrival for use in off-road recoveries. They have several advantages. They are lighter, stronger, and more flexible. They are a one-piece design, so dropping or losing a screw pin is less likely. They are made from synthetic winch line and are rated just like a winch rope. Quality soft shackles have a band or label that lists the various load and strength ratings. If one does break, its lower weight makes it less dangerous than a flying bow shackle.

However, soft shackles can fray if pulled against a sharp edge. They are not as durable as a bow shackle. Also, they typically cost more.

Store-Bought Traction

If driving alone or with another vehicle that will potentially get stuck too, use traction boards. Traction boards are a great aid in sand, snow, and mud. They can be invaluable if there isn't a winch with a suitable anchor nearby. They are expensive, but they are sturdy with no moving parts.

The most well-known brands are usually the better ones. Do some research and speak to someone who has actually used the brand(s) being considered. The design of some brands features a shovel or scoop at the end of the boards. A small square-tip shovel with a short D-handle seems to work the best at clearing the sand, snow, or mud from in front of the tires as well as whatever is dragging underneath.

It is important to shove the tip of the board as far under the tire as possible. This allows the tire to grip the teeth on the board. The board will likely stick up at an angle. This is okay.

Winching

When asked what the first purchase that a new 4WD owner should make, my standard answer is "training." With training, you'll learn about your vehicle, how to drive it, and the terrain you will be traveling over. You'll learn how to avoid getting stuck and how to get unstuck safely.

RECOVERY

Training will also provide information on all kinds of things on which more money can be spent. It can be overwhelming and expensive. Prioritizing the list based on needs and budget is a good idea. Sorting wants from needs can be tough.

Skid plates and rock sliders will prevent damage on rocky trails. However, on sand, mud, and snow, having a quality winch, winch plate, and sturdy front bumper is a good place to start.

We already discussed using a Hi-Lift jack to lift a tire and adding rocks or other material under the tire to gain traction. In a pinch, the Hi-Lift jack can be used as a manual winch. It is not easy, but it does work. Additional gear is needed for this to work.

Removing the jack's foot and attaching a chain or a winch extension rope at each end can move a stuck vehicle up to 4 feet before having to lower the lifting mechanism, take up the slack, and repeat the process. Attaching the jack's top clamp to a tree or other sturdy anchor on one end and attaching the lifting mechanism to the stuck vehicle can pull the stuck vehicle a few inches with each stroke of the Hi-Lift jack's handle.

It can be a substantial investment, but a winch will almost always get a vehicle unstuck. A winch can do amazing things if used properly. Having another driver on the trail with a winch really helps too.

Winches have been around since before 4WD vehicles were invented, and they have served a variety of uses. A winch is a powerful tool that needs to be used carefully. There are plenty of stories and videos that show the damage and injuries from improper use.

Always wear loose-fitting leather-palmed gloves before, during, and after use of a winch. If a cable has a broken strand, it can catch a glove and pull it off rather than injure your hand or pull it into the fairlead.

Early Jeeps had power takeoff (PTO) winches for agricultural use. Hydraulic winches were issued to some HMMWVs in the military. Electric winches are the ones most

Traction boards are a great tool when you are on soft ground without a suitable winch point. Although most people think of them being used in sand, they work well in snow or mud too.

CHAPTER 6

Some traction boards have one end designed to use as a shovel. They are a bit long and can be awkward to use this way, but they work. Having a small shovel along may be a better idea. (Photo Courtesy Adventure Imports)

Traction boards need to have the tips up so that the tire can grip the teeth. That's easy when used with the front tires, but getting them under the rear tires can be a bit harder due to the rocker panels. (Photo Courtesy Adventure Imports)

commonly found on recreational vehicles today.

There are countless electric winch options available today. The rule of thumb is to buy a winch rated for at least one and a half times the weight of your vehicle. If the SUV weighs 5,000 pounds, consider a winch that is rated for at least 7,500 pounds. The extra capacity will pull a stuck vehicle out of deep sand, snow, or mud. Most automotive winches range in capacity from 8,000 to 12,500 pounds. Heavy pickup trucks or HMMWVs may need the 12,500-pound winch.

So, how does one filter through all of the available options. The first thing to consider is how often the winch will be used. No one knows for sure, but the more often the vehicle is out on the trails, the more likely a winch will be needed, even if it's to help someone else.

The next consideration is whether the vehicles will be out in remote areas alone or surrounded by others on a group ride. In other words, how badly will the winch be needed.

Essentially, the answers to these questions come back to quality. If you ride often and sometimes go to remote areas, get a quality winch that is reliable. If the vehicle seldom goes out and then only in a group, it may be possible to get away with a lesser-quality winch.

There are certain winch brands that have been around for 50 years or so, such as Warn, Superwinch, and Ramsey. These companies have changed owners over the years, but their products are considered to be good. The other brands vary in quality but are generally designed to a lower standard (and price). Do your research, read reviews, and ask questions at off-road 4WD shops.

RECOVERY

Today's 4WD vehicles are more capable and complicated than ever before. They are awesome once you know when and how to use their off-road features. The cost of a class with a certified 4WD trainer is usually less than the deductible for your car or health insurance.

When all else fails, use a Hi-Lift jack for manual winching. However, additional equipment is needed to make that work. The Hi-Lift Jack Company makes an off-road kit to help do this.

Winches are a great tool and work when other methods fail. It is important to wear loose-fitting, leather-palmed gloves to protect your hands from broken strands in a winch cable or from rope burns with a synthetic line.

CHAPTER 6

A winch is strongest at the first layer of cable or rope nearest the drum. If the winch is rated for a 9,500-pound pull, it will only pull that much when most of the winch line is spooled out. Each additional layer of winch line on the drum increases the diameter of the drum but reduces the winch's pulling capacity by about 10 percent.

One thing to be aware of is that some winches will respool the winch line faster than others when they are under no load. A winch that has a fast "no load speed" will continue to run for a while after the remote control switch is released. Plan ahead and release the switch a little early to allow for the delay.

When making a winch-buying decision, consider how the winch's functions will be controlled. For decades, the industry standard has been a wired remote control.

However, in an effort to add new technology, some winch manufacturers are offering wireless remote controls using specialized wireless devices or phone apps. Of course, battery-operated remotes and phones can fail if the batteries are weak or dead.

Winch Lines: Steel Cable versus Synthetic Rope

Electric winches are sold with either a galvanized steel aircraft-grade cable or a synthetic rope. A winch with steel cable is often considerably less expensive than one with a synthetic rope.

Steel winch cable has advantages and disadvantages. Steel cables are very durable. They can drag along

The most direct way to control a winch is with a wired remote. A simple switch uses electricity from the winch to pull the winch line in or out.

Steel cables are rugged and can be used in areas where the cable will rub against rocks and trees. However, they are stiff and heavy. The strands of the cable can break over time and hurt your hands if they aren't protected with leather-palmed gloves. Cables are cheaper than synthetic rope and have been in use for decades.

While we all like new technology, it is sometimes better to stay with tried-and-true equipment so that it works reliably when it is needed. New and improved may turn out to be new but not refined. Relying on devices with little batteries can be frustrating, especially if they are only used occasionally.

the ground or over rocks with little or no damage. They are also less expensive to buy or replace than synthetic rope.

However, steel cables do not like to be wound tightly around a winch drum. That tension can cause the outer strands to break and create burrs that can injure bare hands. This is why leather-palmed gloves must be worn. Steel cable can also twist, kink, and flatten when under pressure. It is considerably heavier than rope too. This makes a difference when

Synthetic winch ropes are very flexible and lightweight. Their light weight makes them safer when they break because they store very little energy. However, they are easily abraded or frayed. Rubbing against rocks and trees will damage them. It is important to still wear gloves when using them to protect your hands from rope burns or thorns. Synthetic rope costs two to three times as much as steel cable.

A typical winch line ranges from 80 to 100 feet long. That's ideal as long as a strong anchor point can be found within that distance. If not, having a 50-foot winch line extension along can make a big difference. It can greatly expand the options when doing a recovery of your vehicle or someone else's.

Synthetic winch ropes have many advantages, but one of their weaknesses is that they are easily frayed or cut when there is abrasion. Having a chafe guard protects the rope from abrasion and gives the winch rope a longer life.

pulling the winch line out during a recovery.

Although winch lines seldom break, they can hurt or kill people when they do. A steel cable's weight gives off a lot of energy when it breaks. The cable will whip and damage the vehicle or hurt people who are within its range. It is essential that bystanders stay at least 1.5 times the cable length away. So, if the winch has 100 feet of cable, people and pets need to stay at least 150 feet away.

Synthetic winch ropes have their advantages and disadvantages too. Winch ropes originated in the sailing and fishing industries. They are made from high modulus polyethylene (HMPE) fibers. They weigh very little and even float in water.

The lower weight also makes them safer to use during recoveries. If an HMPE winch rope breaks, it has less stored energy and does less damage when it recoils. Some people say that a winch rope flutters to the ground when it breaks. That's not true. It is typically under thousands of pounds of tension when it breaks, and it will recoil. However, it's lighter weight means that it snaps and falls quicker than a steel cable. Winch rope is also stronger than a

Roller fairleads are preferred because the rollers move with the winch line when pressure is put on them. Hawse fairleads create drag and friction when winch ropes rub on them.

Stretching a cable or a rope under tension allows you to evenly wind the line onto the drum. When done correctly, it prevents the cable or rope from getting tangled. In addition, when under load, using the correct procedure prevents the line from potentially wedging in a lower layer. It also allows the line to be unspooled easily when needed.

RECOVERY

It is always best to secure the winch remote wire so that it can't get caught by a spinning tire and ripped out of the solenoid box. Putting the wire under a hood catch or wrapping it around the driver's mirror will prevent damage to the winch remote.

steel cable when compared in the same diameter.

If winching on a trail and the winch rope breaks, a knot can be tied in it and it will still have roughly 50 percent or more of its rated strength. The winch rope will need to be spliced or replaced when back at the shop.

Winch ropes can be repaired by splicing the two pieces back together using a fid. Another alternative is to add a thimble or an eye to each end of a broken rope and make it into a winch line extension. This can be helpful if reaching for anything beyond the length of the winch's cable or rope.

Winch ropes don't twist, kink, deform, or splinter with sharp burrs. However, it is still a good idea to wear leather-palmed gloves to prevent rope burns. Winch ropes don't rust.

The primary disadvantages for winch ropes are that they are susceptible to damage from abrasion and friction. They are also considerably more expensive to purchase than a steel cable.

Synthetic winch ropes are typically sold with a chafe guard that is loose and slides over the rope to protect it. If it is clear that the winch rope is going to rub on anything once it is set up for recovery, slide the chafe guard to that spot to protect the rope.

Synthetic winch ropes can also be damaged by the heat. Some winches use a brake within the winch drum that gets warm when winching out under power. Some winch ropes now use a heat-treated rope for the first few feet to protect the rope. Some winch manufacturers have also moved the brake outside of the drum.

The most common source of heat is friction. Winch ropes do not like to be rubbed against anything when under tension. Virtually all winch manufacturers include aluminum hawse fairleads with their synthetic rope–equipped winches.

As a winch rope rubs along the aluminum fairlead when being spooled in or out under tension, heat develops due to the friction. A roller fairlead prevents this problem.

By the way, it is normal for a winch rope to fade in color when exposed to the sun, and with use the rope may get fuzzy. Neither of these conditions weaken it. These ropes are commonly exposed to the sun and UV rays on fishing and sailing boats. The color of the rope is irrelevant.

Related Parts Considerations

Once a winch is chosen, consider what else is required. Does the truck or SUV have a sturdy steel front bumper or a plastic bumper? Obviously, a plastic bumper will need to be replaced to support the weight of the winch and the pull it can create. Factor in the cost of a steel (or aluminum) front bumper.

But wait, there's more. In most instances, a winch plate is required to attach the winch to the frame or bumper. Virtually all winches use the same 4.5-inch x 10-inch bolt pattern, so most winches will bolt to nearly all winch plates. All of a sudden, the cost of adding a winch goes up when a new bumper and winch plate are included.

Carefully consider which front bumper suits your style and needs. There are thousands of front bumpers available. Some mount the winch on top, making it easily accessible. Be aware that some bumpers mount the winch very low behind the bumper's face.

This may result in better aerodynamics and airflow into the grille, but those benefits are offset by the fact that it can be difficult to see

CHAPTER 6

It may be good to practice hooking up and operating a winch at home or on the trail when you're not actually stuck. It will be a lot less stressful than waiting until you need help.

Ideally, the truck or SUV should point toward the anchor point so that the winch line doesn't pile up on one end of the drum or the other. If the winch line does pile up, turn the clutch handle to free spool and pull out some line. Then, engage the clutch lever and spool the slack line onto the center of the drum. Be sure that the vehicle can't move while doing this.

When stuck, connect the winch hook or thimble to a tree-saver strap and a shackle. If hooking up to another vehicle, attach the winch hook or thimble directly to their tow point.

the winch line on the drum. Hidden winch bumpers make it nearly impossible to properly respool the winch line after it has been used. It will result in all kinds of loops and tangles that can damage a cable and prevent the line from smoothly pulling out the next time it is needed.

Under Pressure

With a brand-new winch, wrap the winch line under tension. This makes sure that the winch line (cable or rope) is tightly and evenly wound on the drum. This prevents the winch line from getting pinched between gaps in the lower layers. Although the winch may have come from the factory with the winch line neatly wrapped on the drum, it hasn't been wound under tension.

Take the vehicle out to a flat, open area to respool the line under a load. Turn the winch's clutch lever to "free spool" and unwind the winch line, leaving only 7 to 10 wraps on the drum.

Pull the winch line out straight ahead of the vehicle and attach it to an anchor point or another vehicle (using a tree-saver strap if anchored to a tree). Partially engage the parking brake to add resistance.

Now, be sure that the vehicle is running and the transmission is in neutral. Turn the winch clutch handle to "engaged" and insert the winch remote-control plug into the winch's receptacle, being sure that

RECOVERY

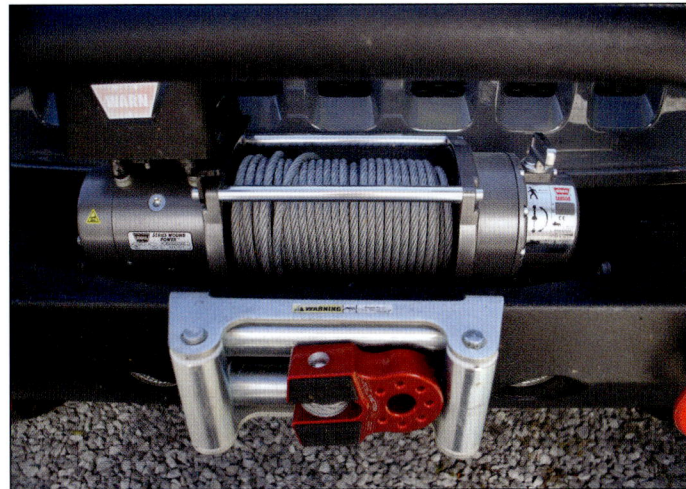

Thimbles on the end of a winch line have become popular. That is because they have a closed hole for the shackle pin to pass through, and that makes a secure connection.

Always keep five wraps of winch line on the drum to provide grip and to prevent the winch line from being pulled off the drum.

If there isn't a sturdy winch point within reach, a land anchor, such as this Pull Pal, can save the day. The ground needs to be soft enough for the plow to dig in but firm enough to provide resistance. It is a good idea to tie a small rope to the plow to help pull it out after the vehicle has been recovered.

THE ULTIMATE OFF-ROAD DRIVER'S GUIDE

Hand Signals

Winch lines and gear came from the rigging industry and so do the hand signals that we use to communicate with the person holding the winch remote control. These same hand signals are used by crane operators and ground personnel. This hand signal means to winch in. This tells the winch operator to pull in the cable.

This hand signal means to winch out. It tells the winch operator to power out the cable.

This hand signal means stop. It tells the winch operator to stop using the winch remote switch.

This hand signal means to bump it. This tells the winch operator to use the winch remote switch quickly and then immediately stop. This causes the winch cable to move just a little bit.

This hand signal means to not operate the winch. This tells the winch operator that your hands will be working around the winch and cable. Any movement of the cable could cause injury.

RECOVERY

the pins are aligned. Route the winch remote cable away from the tire or other moving parts. Wrap the remote cable once around the side mirror, and hand the controller through the window to the driver.

This is a good time to put on some gloves. Slowly run the winch line in while watching it wrap on the drum. Keep your hands away from the fairlead but, if needed, guide the winch line as it winds evenly across the drum. Stop winching when you're down to about the last 6 feet of line. Then, disconnect from the anchor and grab the hook or thimble to slowly spool in the last bit of line.

The winch line can be unspooled and cleaned at home, if necessary. Cleaning a synthetic winch rope basically means washing it off gently with a garden hose. If the synthetic rope has mud, dirt, or sand embedded between the strands, remove it from the drum and wash it in a bucket of gentle detergent. Then, rinse the rope thoroughly and lay it out to dry. This technique also works with recovery straps or ropes.

Now What?

There is no way to properly convey all of the situations in which a winch can help. There are many ways to safely use a winch to help get out of these situations, especially if you have some basic recovery gear.

We will cover some common uses of an electric winch for off-road recovery. Most winch manufacturers provide a training booklet or online video to demonstrate how to safely operate their winches, but this is not a substitute for proper training and hands-on practice.

Once it has been decided that it's time to use a winch, plan what you're going to do and consider if it's safe. Take a deep breath and think about it. If possible, get out and look at the situation. Form a plan and explain that plan to the person hooking up the winch.

Consider where the truck should end up. Is it best to go directly ahead or should someone behind you pull you back?

If you are the stuck driver, your passenger or another driver needs to pull out the winch line and make the connection to a suitable anchor point. That person needs to understand how to operate your winch. You'll need to be able to hand them the tree-saver strap, shackle, and winch remote control. Remember, they need to be wearing loose-fitting leather-palm gloves to protect their hands.

Look for the best anchor point. "Best" means an anchor that is sturdy enough and well located. Vehicles can be moved, but trees can't. Will the anchor point resist the pull you are about to place on it? Check to see if the tree is alive. Look for leaves or pine needles. It's embarrassing to pull a dead tree down onto your truck.

Trees seldom grow in the middle of a trail, so some pulls are at an angle. Try to minimize that angle so that the winch line doesn't pile up on one end of the drum.

Hooking Up

For a typical single-line pull, wrap the tree-saver strap around the tree near the base for maximum strength. Tree-saver straps are webbed straps that are designed to spread the load from the winch to protect the tree's bark. Protecting the tree's bark is essential to keep the tree alive. You never know who else may need a good anchor point in the future. Tree-saver straps are usually 3 to 4 inches wide and 6 to 10 feet long.

A shackle connects the looped ends of the tree-saver strap and gives you a place to connect the winch hook or thimble. If using a bow shackle, the bow should connect the looped ends of the strap, and the pin should be facing out for the hook or thimble.

If using a winch hook, have the tip facing up. If the hook were to break, the energy would be directed down into the ground, not up in the air. Winch hooks are typically removable, and you may want to replace them with a thimble. A thimble is generally considered safer than a hook because it is more securely attached.

Another thing to consider is the distance of the anchor point. Ideally, after pulling most of the winch line out, there still should be at least five to seven wraps on the drum. Those wraps grip the drum and prevent the winch line from being pulled off.

CHAPTER 6

Trying to pull out a heavy vehicle with a lightweight vehicle can be entertaining but not very effective. A winch will just pull you toward the stuck vehicle. Secure the tail end of the light vehicle to a sturdy anchor point to use the full power of the winch.

Winch dampers have been considered a good safety measure for many years. However, in practice, they can get hung up and be pulled into a fairlead. No one should have to go in and move a damper with the winch line under load. The safest option is to simply keep bystanders at least 150 feet away. (Photo Courtesy Jealynn Hedzik)

82 THE ULTIMATE OFF-ROAD DRIVER'S GUIDE

If there isn't a suitable tree within reach, connect the winch line to another vehicle. Be sure to connect the winch hook or thimble to a frame-mounted tow point. If the anchor point is too far way, what else is available that is rated for the pull? A winch line extension? A recovery strap?

If using a winch and driving off-road in areas where trees are scarce, a land anchor may be useful. This will provide an anchor point in places where trees and other vehicles are too far to reach. There are a few brands available, but they have the same function. This is another time that it is wise to get the best quality product you can. One advantage is that they can be placed wherever the soil is soft enough for them to bury and provide the resistance that is needed to pull yourself out.

Once hooked up, the person assisting needs to communicate to the driver with hand signals. The spotter can see everything and signal to the driver when to start and stop winching.

The hand signals tell the driver to "winch in," "winch out," "stop," and more.

Practical Advice

Keep basic recovery gear within reach so that it can be handed out the window. That may mean getting a small canvas bag or something to hold a tree-saver strap, a shackle, and the winch remote. If you always ride with a passenger, store the kit on the passenger's side. This small kit may fit under a seat, beside the driver's seat, or behind the center console. If it can't be reached, the winch may not be able to be used.

What other recovery gear should be on board? Well, that depends on where you wheel and the difficulty level. In general, carry at least one 30-foot recovery strap or rope with a pair of shackles. A receiver hitch pin is a good idea in case a receiver hitch needs to be used to anchor one end of the strap or rope.

For winching, carry two 3- to 4-inch tree-saver straps and a pulley. Always have a pair or two of gloves. A few extra shackles can be helpful sometimes as well. If trees or other anchor points are far apart, a winch line extension can give another 50 feet of reach.

Having a shovel and a jack can certainly help. If driving on sand, snow, or mud, carry a pair of traction

If it is necessary to get from one side of a slack winch line to the other, go around or step on the winch line as you cross over. If you straddle the winch line and the stuck vehicle moves, that winch line will become taut and could seriously affect your odds of becoming a parent.

Neatly spooling the winch cable or rope on the drum isn't about making it look pretty. It's about being sure it will unspool smoothly when it is needed. If a winch line gets tangled, it won't pull out when you're stuck and really need it. It's worth taking the time at home to practice spooling a winch line. It will be much faster and easier if you have that skill.

A winch can do far more than get a vehicle unstuck. It can also move around heavy objects. For example, moving a fallen tree off the trail is easier and often faster than cutting it up with a chainsaw and rolling the logs away.

boards. Be aware that muddy traction boards can be a challenge to store in an SUV. Having a heavy-duty trash bag may be handy for muddy boots, straps, and traction boards.

There will always be more gear to buy and carry, but these items will get you out of most recovery situations. Keep in mind that other people on the ride will carry recovery gear too. It makes it far easier to know what gear belongs to whom if you mark your items.

Caring for your gear will make it last longer and perform better when it is needed. Lubricating a Hi-Lift jack will allow it to work properly, and cleaning mud or debris from a winch rope will make it last longer. They are expensive to replace.

Doing It Right

When winching another vehicle out, be sure that your vehicle is heavier than theirs or that yours is

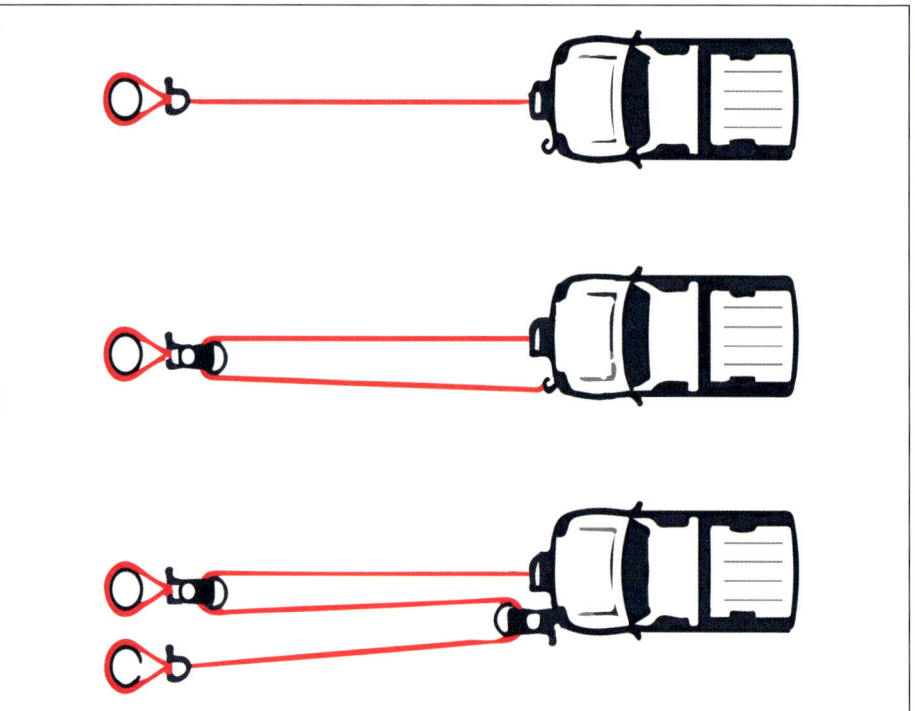

There are times when you may get badly stuck or find someone else who is, or you may want to move a very heavy object. Using the double-line technique doubles a winch's power and takes a lot of stress off the winch. A winch at full load creates a lot of heat and drains the battery quickly. Be kind to your winch, and it will live to pull another day.

well anchored. Otherwise, you will pull yourself toward the stuck vehicle rather than pulling it toward you. Secure your truck to another vehicle or a tree behind you to create a sturdy anchor point.

A winch can draw up to 450 electrical amps when pulling hard. That will drain a battery quickly. Have the engine running, if possible, during winching to recharge the battery.

Winches will also get hot when used hard; they are designed for intermittent use. On long recoveries, you may have to stop and let the winch cool off before winching again. Lessening the load will help. If possible, help the winch by trying to drive forward gently. Clearing sand, snow, or mud away from the undercarriage will lessen the drag. Having another driver hook up and use their winch will split the load as well.

Historically, the rule of thumb was to lay a winch damper or jacket over the winch line to lessen the whipping motion if the line breaks. Now, some people feel that this increases the danger. Winch dampers often travel along with the winch line and get drawn into the fairlead. This means that someone needs to come over beside a cable under tension to move the damper away. This could be dangerous. We want to keep people away from a loaded winch. If everyone stands back one and a half times the length of the winch line, they are out of harm's way and a damper is not needed.

If a winch cable or rope is lying on the ground and you need to cross over it, step on it. Don't straddle a slack winch line. If anything shifts, that cable or rope could become taut and injure sensitive body parts.

After winching, it may be necessary to respool the winch line in a hurry, but try to be as neat as possible so that the winch line doesn't get tangled. It may be needed again soon.

If the winch cable or rope isn't spooled neatly, it can get bound up and won't unspool easily when it is needed again. It can be a bad feeling when your partner is pulling out winch line and it suddenly stops because it's tangled. If this happens, attach the hook or thimble to another vehicle and pull the winch line out gently. It's not always convenient, but it's the only way to untangle a winch line.

Getting Geometrical

One of the cool things that a winch can do is move things around. Using a pulley can redirect the winch's pull. Imagine that you come up to a tree across the trail. Let's assume that you don't have a chainsaw to cut it up and that it's too big to drive over but you can winch it out of the way.

The first thing to consider is which way to move it. The best method is to attach the winch to the base of the tree and pull from there so that all the branches follow. There is less drag that way.

Wrap a tree-saver strap around the tree trunk and add a shackle for the winch hook or thimble. Then, walk away from the tree trunk the same distance as the height of the tree. That will pull the tree far enough to completely get it off the trail.

At the correct distance, find a sturdy tree and attach a tree-saver strap, a shackle, and a pulley. It may be best to wrap the tree-saver strap a bit higher on the tree than normal to help lift the dead tree as it is pulled. This may help create less drag.

Turn your vehicle to aim the winch at the pulley. This creates a straight pull and avoids having the winch line pile up on one side of the drum.

Now, pull the winch line through the pulley and attach it to the tree-saver strap on the tree trunk. Be sure that your vehicle is running and well anchored.

Another time to use this redirect technique is when a vehicle slips off the edge of the trail. Use two winching vehicles to pull the truck sideways back onto the trail by attaching the winch lines to the front and rear tow points and pulling together.

If you are pulling a heavy load with the winch and think the weight may be too much, use a technique called "double lining." This involves spooling the winch line out to an anchor point, through a pulley, and then back to the vehicle's tow point. Doing this doubles the pulling power of the winch but cuts the speed in half. It's a slow but powerful way to move a heavy load.

Be aware that with additional recovery gear and advanced training, you can create triple-line winch pulls or a Spanish Burton rig that quadruples a winch's pulling ability. These techniques, and the gear that they require, may be beyond what the average 4WD driver will need on the trail, but it never hurts to know more.

There are many quality recovery products available to help one get unstuck, and there are a few low-quality products that may be dangerous. There are also some interesting gadgets that don't seem to solve any problems but look good.

When considering what to buy, ask yourself if you actually need it, if it is of high quality, and if it is safe. If you are uncertain, find a certified 4WD trainer or a trusted person with hands-on recovery experience.

CHAPTER 7

Four-Wheel Drive

All-wheel drive (AWD) is a drivetrain optimized for on-road use in slippery conditions. It has the capability to send the engine's power to all four tires all of the time. When a tire slips or spins, the computer instantly applies the brakes to that wheel and shifts the power to the tires that have a better grip. On snowy or wet roads, it helps keep your vehicle moving forward better than front-wheel drive or rear-wheel drive.

However, the biggest limitation of AWD is the lack of a low-range transfer case. This missing component prevents AWD cars from climbing steep hills over rough terrain. The low-range transfer case can triple the amount of torque (power) being sent to the wheels. A typical AWD car or SUV has low ground clearance and small tires. In addition, the suspension is designed for relatively smooth dirt or paved roads.

AWD systems either use a center differential or a clutch-pack coupling between the front and rear axles to allow the front and rear tires to spin at different speeds. Many AWD systems seamlessly transfer torque between the front and rear tires (as needed) and automatically switch into two-wheel drive when AWD is not needed to improve fuel economy.

All-wheel drive can be used on dry pavement with no ill effects because it is engineered to enable each tire to rotate at its own speed in turns (inboard tires rotate slower in corners), so AWD is a better system than 4WD for the average driver who wants additional traction. For this reason, AWD is found on many modern SUVs and passenger cars.

Vintage 4WD

Historians have various ideas about the first true 4WD vehicle, but

All-wheel drive (AWD) has improved and become more popular over the years. It works well on wet or snowy paved roads and shifts power to the tires with grip, as needed. Virtually all AWD vehicles are cars, SUVs, or minivans. Some performance cars have begun using AWD to provide maximum grip. These vehicles typically have low ground clearance, small tires, and limited wheel travel. They are not engineered for off-road use. (Photo Courtesy Photo-Denver/Shutterstock.com)

FOUR-WHEEL DRIVE

Although early 4WD vehicles were built in small numbers going back as far as 1903. It was World War II that launched the mass production of jeeps and 4WD trucks. Soldiers who drove them realized the benefits on the muddy roads and fields of Europe. This image shows the Bantam factory in Butler, Pennsylvania. (Photo Courtesy Omix/Truck Hero)

When they came home, many soldiers bought 4WD jeeps and trucks for use on their farms and ranches. In time, people began driving them for recreation. Clubs were formed, events were held, competitive races were staged, and remote areas were explored. These vehicles literally created a whole new lifestyle and spurred aftermarket accessory sales. (Photo Courtesy Omix/Truck Hero)

CHAPTER 7

The military jeeps that were built during World War II by Willys and Ford always had the front axles and driveline engaged. The only thing that changed was whether the driver moved the shift lever between 2WD or 4WD.

many credit the Dutch 1903 Spyker with that title. It was the world's first 4WD car that was directly powered by an internal combustion engine, and it was the first with a front-engine 4WD layout. It was commissioned for the Paris to Madrid race of 1903.

Designs for 4WD in America came from the Twyford Company of Brookville, Pennsylvania. Six vehicles were made there around 1906, and one still exists.

The first 4WD vehicles to go into mass production were built by the American Four-Wheel Drive Auto Company (FWD) of Wisconsin, which was founded in 1908. These trucks were primarily used by military forces in World War I.

The American Marmon-Herrington Company was founded in 1931 to serve a growing market for moderately priced 4WD vehicles. Marmon-Herrington specialized in

Manual locking hubs allowed 4WD owners to unlock the hubs and drive in 2WD without the front driveline spinning. This reduces maintenance on the front driveline and improves fuel mileage. However, it can be inconvenient to get in and out of the vehicle to lock or unlock the hubs. So, manual locking hubs are rarely seen on modern 4WD vehicles. (Photo Courtesy Warn Industries)

Early gear-driven transfer cases often had twin-sticks to shift between 2WD and 4WD and between high-range and low-range gears. Modern 4WDs now use a single lever to shift the transfer case, and some manufacturers are using push buttons or knobs to electronically shift the transfer case.

Early military vehicles were designed for slow-speed convoys and off-road travel. Early civilian 4WD vehicles were more suited for agricultural use. In the 1950s and 1960s, America's need for speed increased, the slow 4WD jeeps and trucks were being left behind. To drive safely and not over-rev the engine, overdrive units were developed and added behind the transmission to provide another gear. (Photo Courtesy Omix/Truck Hero)

converting Ford trucks to four-wheel drive.

The World War II jeep, which was originally developed by American Bantam but mass-produced by Willys and Ford, became the best-known 4WD vehicle in the world during the war. The American Dodge WC series and Chevrolet G506 4x4 trucks were also mass-produced. In the end, North America built about 1.5 million 4x4 vehicles during the war.

After the war, 4WD trucks became more popular with civilians due to their all-weather capabilities. Many roads in America were still dirt in the 1940s and 1950s. Rural citizens needed to get around on their farms and ranches, and people needed to get to town to shop or conduct business.

Military jeeps used during World War II had the front axle's hubs engaged all the time. In 2WD, this caused the front axle shafts, differentials, and front driveshaft to spin. However, no power was applied to the front tires. When the driver wanted to engage 4WD, all that he or she had to do was move one of the transfer-case levers to shift into 4WD.

After the war, many of the 4WD vehicles that were built for the civilian market used manual locking front hubs. This allowed them to "free-wheel" on paved roads, which produced less wear on the rotating driveline and improved fuel economy. The downside was that the driver had to get out to "lock-in" the hubs before proceeding on dirt roads or trails. This can be a messy job if it's muddy, raining, or snowing when 4WD is desired. The hubs were typically "unlocked" when returning to dry pavement.

Early military and civilian Jeeps used a twin-stick transfer case so that the driver used one stick (lever) to shift from 2WD to 4WD and back. The other stick (lever) was used to shift between high-range and low-range gears in the transfer case.

Some owners remove a pin in the transfer case to allow them to use 2WD and low-range gears at the same time. Others engage 4WD low range with the transfer case levers but leave the front axle hubs unlocked. This achieves the same result.

While many owners bought 4WD vehicles for the low-range abilities, some wanted to go faster too. As roads improved and highways were built, the 4WDs became the leaders

CHAPTER 7

Part-time 4WD means that you decide when to shift into 4WD or out of 4WD. A driver can look ahead and determine whether 4WD is necessary and whether the road or trail surface is slippery enough to require it. 4WD doubles the traction, but it should only be used on dirt trails or slippery paved roads.

Shifting on the fly between 2WD high range (2Hi) and 4WD high range (4Hi) can be done while you're moving because you are using the same high-range gears in the transfer case in both positions. What you're actually doing when you shift into 4Hi is engaging the front driveshaft for extra traction.

of a slow-moving parade. Fellow travelers tried desperately to pass them.

Where there is demand, supply soon follows. Electric and gear-driven overdrive units were built and sold as aftermarket accessories to allow 4WD owners to zip along with their 2WD brethren.

Part-Time 4WD

Traditional part-time four-wheel drive (4WD) is intended only for use off-road or on extremely slippery surfaces. The "part-time" aspect means that the driver must actively shift into four-wheel drive by turning a knob, pushing a button, or yanking a lever.

It's a simpler, more mechanical system that requires the driver to engage it, not a computer. However, four-wheel drive is not designed to be used on dry paved roads and is reserved for vehicles with serious off-road capability.

Engaging the front driveshaft keeps the front and rear axles turning at the same speed. In sand, mud, and snow, this guarantees that, at a minimum, engine torque is always being sent to at least one front and one rear wheel without relying on computers to predict or detect wheel slip.

In a curve, a vehicle's four wheels all rotate at different speeds. You can see this in the tracks left when a vehicle turns through fresh snow or wet sand, as each wheel traces a unique arc with a slightly different radius.

When turning, each tire rotates at a different speed and in a different arc. The tires on the inside of the turn pivot, while the outer tires have to travel farther and faster to catch up. (Photo Courtesy sylv1rob1/Shutterstock.com)

THE ULTIMATE OFF-ROAD DRIVER'S GUIDE

On low-grip surfaces, such as sand, snow, ice, dirt, or mud, drivetrain binding isn't a problem because the tires that travel farther or faster can slip or spin a little to catch up.

The huge advantage that any 4WD system has is the ability to use a lower set of gears within the transfer case. 4WD transfer cases have a high-range and low-range set of internal gears.

When you leave dry paved roads and start driving on dirt, it's common practice to shift the transfer case from 2WD high range into 4WD high range as you are moving. This is known as "shifting on the fly." This feature allows the front driveshaft and wheels to be engaged seamlessly. It also gives more traction and control. Having the front tires pulling provides a better grip on loose surfaces and helps pull the vehicle around curves. This is especially helpful on gravel roads where it may feel like you're driving on marbles. Shifting back and forth between 2WD high and 4WD high range can be done in motion because you are still using the same set of gears inside the transfer case.

However, a section of rough road or an off-road trail requires slow speed and extra power. Shift into that powerful set of low-range gears. This is what most people think of when describing 4WD. Once you shift, you will have monster truck power with tractor speed.

To shift into 4WD low range, come to a complete stop. Then, shift the transmission into neutral. This takes the pressure off the transfer case gears and allows them to move without grinding. Finally, use the knob or lever to shift into the "4Lo" position. The shift pattern will vary from vehicle to vehicle, but the pattern will be on the shift knob or button.

The 4WD transfer case shifter may need to be tugged on to get it to move into the 4Lo position, especially with new vehicles that haven't had the transfer case used much. When pushing a 4WD button, it may take a minute to engage. In most cases, there is a light in the instrument cluster that shows when it has been shifted.

Be aware that when you are ready to speed up on dirt or return to paved roads, you'll need to stop again, shift the transmission into neutral, and move the 4WD knob or button back into the 4WD high or 2WD high range. Of course, this shifts the transfer case back into the high-range gears.

While driving in 4Lo, pressure may build on the low-range gears,

Shifting between 4WD high range and 4WD low range requires coming to a complete stop, shifting the transmission into neutral, and then selecting the 4Lo position with the transfer case lever or knob. New vehicles that haven't been shifted into 4WD very often may find that it takes extra effort to shift the transfer-case lever. If your vehicle uses a 4WD knob on the dash, it may take a few seconds to actually shift. The 4Lo light in the dash may blink until it shifts and then shine steadily. (Photo Courtesy Basel Al Seoufi/Shutterstock.com)

Once you've shifted into 4Lo, you may see a light illuminate in your instrument cluster to verify that you really are in 4WD low range. Then, you can shift the transmission into drive or select your own gear if you have a manual transmission. You will know immediately if you have successfully shifted due to the extra torque and very slow speed.

CHAPTER 7

making it difficult to shift back to the high-range gearset. Pulling firmly on the transfer-case shift lever may help. Other tricks to release the pressure may involve backing up or driving forward slowly while turning the wheels back and forth. Then, stop and try to shift again. This usually works.

When you are successful, the 4WD light goes out in the dash instrument cluster.

A good suggestion is to find a dirt or gravel road and try shifting into and out of 4WD. Use high range and low range to feel the difference. Get comfortable with it before you need it. Bring the owner's manual or an "old timer" along if you need to.

Full-Time 4WD

Why would you want 4WD on full time, instead of just turning it on when needed? The primary reason is improved handling. Having all four wheels moving the truck or SUV allows it to take corners better and provides better directional stability when the vehicle is moving in a steady-state condition. Improved handling in normal driving conditions results in a safer drive.

Another reason for full-time 4WD is convenience. Let's say that you're driving on a road that has segments of ice and snow but is mostly dry. Instead of having to engage and disengage your part-time 4WD when hitting and leaving those slick spots, with the four wheels going all the time, you don't have to think about it. You just drive.

The big downside of full-time 4WD is that it uses much more fuel than part-time 4WD because the engine has to transfer power to all four wheels all the time.

Just as on part-time 4WD vehicles, full-time 4WD vehicles have both a front and rear differential on the front and rear axles that allow the left and right wheels to move at different speeds when making a turn.

So, how do full-time 4WD vehicles avoid drivetrain binding due to the front and rear wheels turning at different speeds? It is done by adding a third differential in the middle of the drivetrain. This center differential is considered to be "open." It allows slippage.

Most of the time, full-time 4WD works pretty much the same way as AWD: the center differential sends engine power to both the front and rear wheels all the time. The center differential allows the front and rear driveshafts to move at different speeds, which allows the vehicle to operate normally even when making turns on dry pavement.

Let's say that you're in a full-time 4WD vehicle with a center open differential. You're driving up your driveway and the front wheels hit a patch of icy snow. Those front wheels have the least amount of traction and represent the path of least resistance. So, the center differential is going to send all of the power to the front wheels, causing them to spin in place while the rear wheels just sit there on dry pavement not moving at all. To get up the driveway, it'd be nice to have those rear wheels getting some power.

To solve this problem, most full-time 4WD vehicles use a limited-slip differential (LSD) or Torsen center differential. These types of center differentials provide the benefit of open center differentials, but when one set of wheels hits a slick spot, instead of sending *all* the power to those spinning wheels, it still sends some of the power to the wheels that are on dry pavement.

Some full-time 4WD vehicles have a locking center differential that's built into the transfer case. When a driver actively engages it, the center differential locks the front and rear driveshafts together so that they turn at the same speed, thus delivering equal amounts of torque to the rear and front wheels. This should only be engaged off-road where the tires can slip a little to compensate for the axle's need to turn at different speeds. Locking the center differential creates a traditional 4WD with a 50-50 split of power to the axles.

The center differential allows the axles to turn at different speeds when necessary and prevents binding. Once locked, you have traditional 4WD with no slippage in the drivetrain. The power is split 50-50 between the front and rear axles. Locking the center differential should only be done off-road or when you have slippery road conditions. (Photo Courtesy Andrew Glushchenko/Shutterstock.com)

THE ULTIMATE OFF-ROAD DRIVER'S GUIDE

CHAPTER 8

MODERN TECHNOLOGY ON 4WD VEHICLES

Modern automotive technology is amazing, and the pace at which technology is evolving is incredible as well. A number of factors are driving these rapid changes, but the primary factor is safety. Many new features are designed to improve safety.

Anti-Lock Braking System

The automotive industry began using anti-lock braking systems (ABS) in the 1970s, but it became more commonplace in the 1990s. Wheel-speed sensors were added to determine if each wheel was turning or not. If not, the computer released the brakes at that wheel to get it turning again and prevent skidding.

ABS is a great safety feature, but drivers need to be aware that ABS does not shorten braking distances. It does, however, allow better steering under hard braking.

Don't be surprised if the ABS light comes on in the instrument cluster while it's active. This warning light should immediately go out when the ABS is no longer active.

Another important thing to know is that ABS offers limited help in snowy or icy conditions. ABS relies on having at least one wheel turning for speed comparison. If all four wheels are locked, the computer thinks that the vehicle is stopped.

Traction Control

While ABS brakes were designed to help a vehicle stop, traction control systems were introduced to help it go. This gives the driver some control over the amount of tire spin. Drivers in 4WD low range can select the type of terrain on which they are driving, and the computer adjusts the amount of tire spin allowed.

Selecting the "rocks" setting allows for relatively little tire spin,

ABS prevents skidding and allows for more steering control under hard braking. This may help a driver avoid hitting something or someone. When applying the brakes hard and activating the ABS, the brake pedal will pulse and make unusual sounds. (Photo Courtesy rumruay/Shutterstock.com)

THE ULTIMATE OFF-ROAD DRIVER'S GUIDE

Early traction control systems were completely controlled by the onboard computer system in the vehicle. The driver had little control over its use. Now, the amount of tire spin can be adjusted before the traction control kicks in. Each manufacturer has its own variety of buttons, knobs, and display menus to change the traction settings. In addition, there is typically an "off" button. (Photo Courtesy otomobil/Shutterstock.com)

Using the traction control "off" button may help maintain momentum in slippery conditions, but stability control is still operating in the background. It may reduce engine power or apply the brakes individually if it determines that driving conditions are unsafe.

Most manufacturers of 4WD vehicles have some form of traction control. It usually has a button to turn it off as well. Some go further and offer a knob or display menu that allows you to select the type of terrain on which you are driving. Then, the computer adjusts the amount of tire spin that it will allow. It can use braking or reduce engine power to slow the spinning tire. Locking differentials "lock" the two axle shafts together, and both tires turn in unison until the locker is turned off.

and selecting "snow" or "sand" allows for a bit more. The "mud" setting allows the most spin. Traction control tries to limit the spinning wheel's speed so that it doesn't overpower the available traction on the ground. Excessive wheel spin won't move a vehicle forward.

If one wheel is spinning faster than the other three wheels, the computer will apply the brakes at that wheel to prevent excessive tire spin. The computer may also decide to reduce engine power to limit wheel spin. This has caused great frustration for 4WD owners who wanted a bit of tire spin in poor traction conditions, such as mud, but found that they suddenly lacked the power to go up a slippery hill. Reducing power and applying brakes in low traction terrain can kill momentum.

Now, most manufacturers have a button on the dash to disengage traction control. When the traction control "off" button is pushed, it disengages the traction control, but stability control will still be active, which can also reduce power, apply braking, etc.

Another traction-enhancing feature that Jeep Wranglers have is known as a "brake lock differential." It controls wheel speed from side to side across the same axle. This is helpful for owners who do not have locking differentials. It is not a substitute for a locking differential, but it helps equalize tire spin. If you've ever gotten stuck on wet grass, you know that one tire can be spinning furiously while the other tire is completely still.

A brake lock differential does not care how fast the wheels are turning, just that they are turning at the same speed. In 4WD high range, turn off the electronic stability control with the ESC button on the dash. This allows the brake lock differential to work. In 4WD low range, the electronic stability control is already off, so the brake lock differential works automatically.

Each manufacturer has a different brand name and method to adjust its proprietary traction control systems. For example, Toyota has TRAC for on-road use and A-TRAC for off-road

Airbags are a proven lifesaver, and there are more of them in trucks than ever. However, there are safety precautions needed for children, especially infants and toddlers. (Photo Courtesy Ivanova Tetyana/Shutterstock.com)

use. An upgrade is its "Multi-Terrain Select" traction control system. Finally, it offers an optional rear locking differential (locker). Toyota uses push buttons and knobs to engage its features and change its settings.

Airbags

Airbags were introduced in the mid-1970s. Initially, they were offered in the steering wheel, and some manufacturers offered a passenger airbag in the dash. The passenger airbag could be turned off by the driver in some vehicles. Today, auto manufacturers offer as many as 10 airbags throughout the cabin. Typically, the front passenger seat has a weight sensor so that the power of the airbag deployment matches the weight of the passenger.

When airbags first became available on 4WD vehicles, there was concern about them going off while bouncing around on off-road trails. Airbag deployment is triggered when sensors feel sudden deceleration. Off-road driving rarely reaches the level of impact required to deploy an airbag.

Radar and Ultrasonic Sensors

Advanced Driver-Assistance Systems (ADAS) is an acronym that you will hear more and more.

At first, we had backup sensors. These small radar or ultrasonic sensors were added to the back bumper to prevent child deaths. Then, blind-spot monitoring was added in the mirrors to track the vehicles beside you. Forward-facing sensors are the key to adaptive braking, adaptive cruise control, forward collision warning, and much more.

Now, cross path detection uses radar in the taillights to detect side-to-side motion. This halo of sensors is bringing us closer and closer to autonomous driving.

Cameras

Once automotive cameras became commonplace, manufacturers began adding them everywhere. Backup cameras came first. The images were routed into large touch screen displays when the vehicle was shifted into reverse.

Lane departure is a safety warning feature that uses a camera mounted

Children and pets have been injured or died from vehicles backing over them. To reduce this tragedy, manufacturers started adding radar sensors in the rear bumper to warn drivers about objects that were too close. That eventually evolved to include backup cameras that display images on a dash display. This has undoubtedly saved lives. A side benefit is that we can more clearly see behind us when backing up off-road.

CHAPTER 8

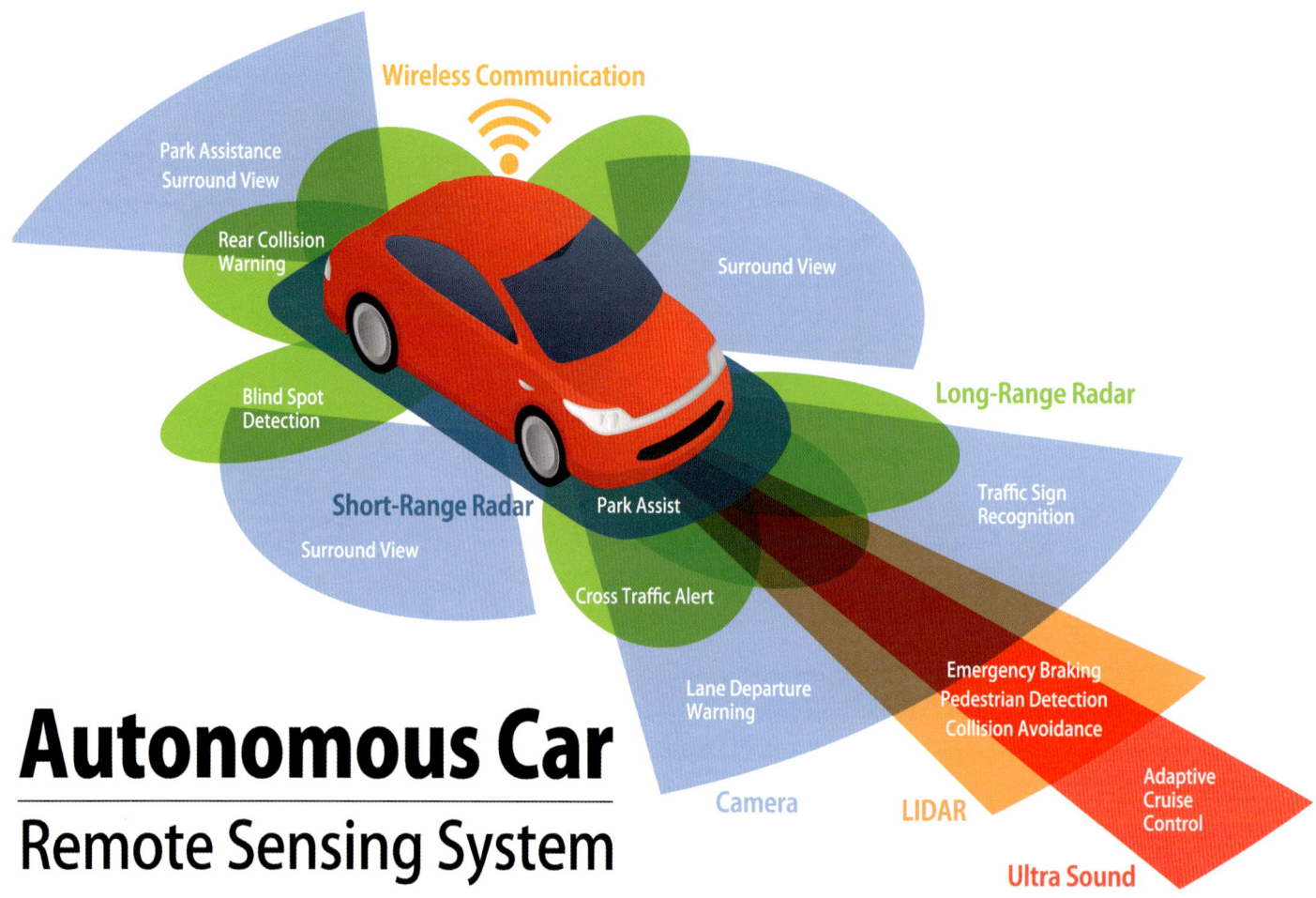

Autonomous Car
Remote Sensing System

Sensors are being added to allow autonomous driving. Radar and Lidar (lasers) measure the distances between your vehicle and obstacles. Cameras monitor and display road features, road signs, pedestrians, and bicyclists. (Photo Courtesy metamorworks/Shutterstock.com)

high behind the windshield to monitor the lines on the road and a vehicle's position relative to them. If the computer thinks that the vehicle is about to cross a lane stripe, it will issue a warning sound.

Now, integrated cameras and radar sensors are going a step further to detect pedestrians and bicyclists in the roadway and warn you. Smart cameras mounted behind the windshield can also detect road signs ahead and display them for you on the dash display.

Jeep has recently introduced an infrared camera for night use to detect deer and pedestrians that a driver might not see.

Off-Road Cameras

Backup cameras work well off-road and can be useful when backing down a hill after a failed hill climb. Toyota and others have added cameras in the side mirrors facing down so that the rocker panels can be seen. Forward-facing trail cameras mounted in the grille have been available for a few years now too.

Some manufacturers are adding cameras mounted under the chassis to monitor what's happening as a vehicle drives over obstacles. While camera images on a display are mesmerizing, don't forget to look up occasionally to see what's happening outside.

Off-Road Cruise Control

4WD manufacturers are now offering off-road cruise control that allows you to set the vehicle's speed

96 THE ULTIMATE OFF-ROAD DRIVER'S GUIDE

Once backup camera systems were added, it became easier to add more cameras for different views. Now, we can find cameras in the side mirrors pointing down to see the rocker panels. Forward-facing cameras in the grille show drivers what is ahead. A camera mounted high behind the windshield can warn drivers about pedestrians and bicyclists in the roadway that they might not see yet. They can even detect roadside signs and display them.

Off-road cruise control is a feature that builds upon the computer-controlled braking systems in modern vehicles. You can set a speed from 1 to 5 mph and take your foot off the gas pedal. This is one less driving task required when driving off-road over rough terrain. A quick tap of the gas pedal or brake pedal will disengage it.

when in 4WD low range. The speeds are usually limited to 5 mph. Toyota has CRAWL Control and Jeep has Selec-Speed Control. Others are sure to follow.

When a driver engages this feature, he or she can focus on steering around or over obstacles. If the driver touches the gas or brake pedals, it disengages.

Hidden Safety Software

Hidden technology, such as stability control, is present in most modern vehicles. It is normally on and operating behind the scenes, using a variety of sensors and computers to control the application of engine power, brakes, etc.

Some manufacturers allow you to fully turn off stability control by pressing and holding a VSC or ESC button. Stability control is a wonderful feature that has undoubtedly saved many lives and vehicles. However, in a few off-road conditions, it can limit forward progress and leave you stuck. If you can anticipate those conditions (usually heavy snow or mud), press and hold the stability control button until the warning light in the instrument cluster tells you that it is off.

Jeep's electronic roll mitigation software senses the potential for wheel lift on turns. Then, the computer will begin applying the brakes on one side of the vehicle or the other to correct understeer or oversteer. This feature has also saved people and vehicles, but it has probably scared a few people when it engages.

Jeep also has its AutoPark feature that automatically shifts the automatic transmission into park if the driver's seat belt is unbuckled, the brake pedal is released, and the

CHAPTER 8

Hill-descent buttons are becoming more common. Typically, the vehicle's computers will selectively apply engine braking or wheel braking to control the speed going down steep hills. This reduces the risk of sliding or skidding. It usually does this faster than a driver can. (Photo Courtesy otomobil/Shutterstock.com)

Satellite navigation can be found on any phone and now it's available in a 4x4. Large displays and satellite maps make it easier than ever to navigate. Just remember that it is only as good as the accuracy of the maps. Each year, there are a few stories about people becoming stranded because they blindly followed their GPS systems.

door is opened with the automatic transmission in gear. This feature is designed to help drivers who forget to shift into park before getting out of the vehicle.

Convenience Features

Some manufacturers are offering hill start assist as a feature. It holds the brakes on the truck for a few seconds when it senses it is stopped facing uphill. This is done to prevent it from rolling backward when the foot is taken off the brake and applied to the gas. It works on both manual- and automatic-transmission vehicles. This feature works equally well on-road and off-road.

Hill descent control usually requires the driver to push a button on the dash to engage it. This feature is designed to allow a smooth and controlled hill descent on steep or slippery hills without the driver needing to touch the brake pedal. This system applies the brakes to each wheel individually, as needed, to slow the descent.

Jeep's tire fill alert software uses the tire pressure monitoring system (TPMS) sensors to notify you when your tire air pressure meets the setting that you selected when airing down tires or airing them back up.

More technology continues to be added each year. Android Auto and Apple Carplay integrate our phones with our vehicles in ways that were unimagined not long ago. Having Wi-Fi in our vehicles is also a step forward. Manufacturers can update a vehicle's software overnight as needed, and you no longer need to have this done at a dealership.

Satellite navigation is another great convenience feature. It can help you find the trailhead, and if you are on public dirt roads, they may appear as well. Being able to find the nearest gas or recharging station, medical care, or dealership can be handy too.

The number of sensors, computers, and features will continue to increase, as will the prices for new vehicles. There is a cost for all of the conveniences and safety options. Car payments can rival rent or mortgage payments for some people.

The real game changer may be when the fully electric vehicles hit the showrooms. They will have incredible torque and sophisticated drive systems. In addition, they will still need a variety of sensors, cameras, and computers to provide traction, stability, and safety.

CHAPTER 9

UPGRADES

Buying any 4WD vehicle is usually just a place to start. It is a platform to take you to your next adventure. The upgrades made should be determined by what you want to do with your truck.

That sounds simple, but it usually isn't. One of the hardest things to do is know what the goals are and then build a vehicle for those purposes. Will it be used for commuting, hunting, fishing, rock crawling, mud running, camping, mountain biking, hiking, or general trail riding? How hardcore do you want to go? Try to be realistic so that you don't buy accessories twice.

Some folks want to outfit their truck to look good on the street or in car shows. Their plans don't include getting it dirty. That's okay. Everyone likes a good-looking truck. Many people buy a great daily commuting vehicle and then add upgrades to make it perform on the weekends.

Life is full of compromises, and that's especially true with your decisions for your vehicle. While the gnarly bias-ply mud tires are awesome off-road, they wear fast and make a lot of noise on the daily commute. The 8 inches of lift looks fantastic, but it totally changes the driving experience. You get the idea.

Many of us are guilty of setting up a suspension lift system for a specific tire size, only to replace it in a few years to add bigger tires.

Conspicuous Consumption

It is not unusual to spends thousands of dollars on wheels, tires, suspension lifts, bumpers, winches, roof racks, roof-top tents, 12-volt refrigerators, skid plates, rock rails, CB or GMRS radios, GPS units, seat covers, and more. A multi-billion-dollar industry offers an incredible array of aftermarket accessories.

Congratulations! After doing your research and taking a test drive, you've bought a 4WD truck or SUV. The next step is to drive it as-is for a little while before deciding what to change or add. Any upgrades will be determined by what you want to do with your truck. Will you be taking weekend trails rides, going backcountry camping, or something else? (Photo Courtesy Betto Rodrigues/Shutterstock.com)

THE ULTIMATE OFF-ROAD DRIVER'S GUIDE

CHAPTER 9

One of the perks of living in the United States is the easy access to off-road accessories, especially if you drive one of the more popular models. There is a multi-billion-dollar industry ready to sell aftermarket accessories. In fact, the choices can be overwhelming. Try to narrow your choices and then try to see the parts in person. Call a local 4WD shop to see if they have what you want in stock. (Photo Courtesy the SEMA Show)

Be aware the more that a 4WD vehicle is modified for off-road use, the less road friendly it may become. If the goal is to have a dual-purpose truck that can still be driven to work or school, then consider compromises with the suspension lift height, tire choices, axle gearing, etc.

With research, most anything you want can probably be found, especially with the more popular trucks and SUVs. Local 4WD shops, online forums, and eCommerce reviews can help you see what's available.

Attending 4WD club rides or off-road events may let you see these accessories in person. Vendors will often attend larger events so that you can speak with a company's representative before investing in new products.

UPGRADES

4WD clubs and off-road events are great places to go window shopping too. The items can be seen firsthand, and there is usually someone to answer questions about it. There may also be new products you didn't know about. The bonus is that you'll probably meet great people. (Photo Courtesy Rugged Ridge/Truck Hero)

When you get stuck alone, you lose many of your best recovery options. Having a recovery strap doesn't help if there is no one to pull you out. Without a second 4WD vehicle, there isn't a mobile anchor point that can be placed where you need it. The trees may not be close enough for the winch line. Also, who will tell campfire stories about your epic adventure if no one is there to witness it? (Photo Courtesy Cheri Alguire/Shutterstock.com)

Having frame-mounted tow points is a huge safety feature. Most 4WD vehicle manufacturers literally bolt their tow points to the frame. That's the sturdiest place to attach a recovery strap or winch hook/thimble. A properly mounted front bumper or rear receiver hitch will also work as long as it is frame mounted. A fully stretched recovery strap or properly rigged winch line creates an incredibly strong pulling force. The tow point must be very strong. Otherwise, someone can get badly hurt. (Photo Courtesy otomobil/Shutterstock.com)

Transport loops are strictly for tying a vehicle down during transport from the port or factory to the dealership where it will be sold. They offer an attachment point to secure the vehicle on a ship, train, or trailer. For example, the Toyota Tacoma can be found with a transport loop on the left frame rail and an optional factory tow hook on the right frame rail.

A common question is "What do I buy first?"

Well, that depends on what the use will be. Skid plates protect the expensive drivetrain if the vehicle will be trail riding or rock crawling. An air compressor and pressure gauge may be the most helpful if driving on soft sand or snow. A pair of rubber boots and a good winch will be needed in the mud.

Seat time and experience will help you determine the upgrades that you'd like to purchase. It may be an air compressor to air up at the end of a trail ride, a sturdy winch bumper and a good winch, or bigger/better tires. There's nothing wrong with any of these choices. The trails and your budget will help you determine what to buy first.

Air Compressors and Tire Deflators

One of the very first things that most drivers do when they leave pavement is reduce the tire pressure. This process is called "airing down." There are a variety of tire gauges and deflators available. Air can be let air out of tires with anything from a pen to a pocketknife. However, a good deflator is a wonderful tool. It allows you to see the tire pressure and easily let more air out. Some deflators can also be connected to an air compressor or carbon dioxide (CO_2) tank to reinflate the tires too. That's even better.

Some drivers rely on others or find a gas station with an air compressor to reinflate their tires. However, before long, many folks want their own portable air compressor or CO_2 tank so that they are more self-reliant. Portable 12-volt air compressors range in quality and price from cheap junk to high-quality units. Most people need something in the middle.

CO_2 tanks can be purchased in various sizes and mounted to roll bars, etc. The advantage is that they can hold a considerable volume of

Partially deflating the tires is known as "airing down." It's one of the first things that most drivers do when driving off-road. It's free and it improves the tire's grip on the ground. There are many ways to air down. Convenience stores have inaccurate pencil-type air pressure gauges. Other options let air out quickly by removing the valve core temporarily. These can be confusing to use, and it is easy to release too much air. One of the best is known as a deflator. It lets air out of the tire in a controlled way and shows the remaining air pressure on an accurate gauge. The best part is that if you have an air compressor, it will let you reinflate the tires using the same gauge.

Airing down works well, but at the end of the trail, the tires need to be reinflated before driving very far on the pavement. Driving partially deflated tires on paved roads at higher speeds will cause the sidewalls to get hot and can lead to a blowout. If you need to drive to the nearest public air compressor, stay at around 45 mph and air up as soon as practical. The better option is to buy a portable air compressor. That way, the tires can be reinflated anywhere to drive safely on paved roads.

UPGRADES

CO_2 and, when released quickly, they can reseat a tire bead that has come off. The main disadvantage is that when they run out of CO_2, they are done. Refilling the tanks can be difficult if you don't live near a welding supply company. Of course, there is a cost to refill the tank each time. Lastly, be aware that CO_2 tanks need to be hydrostatically tested every five years.

Inexpensive air compressors are designed for short use to fill beach balls and pool toys. They are not intended to fill four large off-road tires.

Air compressors have two main features that are the most important: (1) the volume of air that they produce and (2) the length of time that they will run before overheating. Like many things in life, more is better.

Air volume is measured in cubic feet per minute (CFM). Off-road tires have large volumes but need relatively low pressure. Most tire-pressure sensors stop blinking at around 35 psi. So, look for compressors that produce high volumes of air. Typical off-road air compressors will produce between 2 and 6 cfm with no load. They produce less air volume as the tire pressure increases.

The length of time that an air compressor will run before overheating is called a duty cycle. For example, if a portable air compressor will run for 20 minutes before overheating and needing to cool off, but it only takes 15 minutes to fill up the tires to street pressure, then the compressor should fit your needs well. If it only runs for 10 minutes before needing to cool off, you will be sitting around waiting before you can finish airing up and drive home.

Look at online reviews and ask other 4WD owners what they use and what their experience has been with their air compressors. A good air compressor and inflator gauge is a pleasure to use, especially at the end of the day when it's time for dinner or to travel home.

Mild or Wild

Any retail 4x4 shop will say that its bread and butter is selling and installing suspension lifts, new wheels, and taller tires. The truck will look and perform off-road better with these upgrades if they are done right. The key is that they need to be done right.

Modifying or replacing the stock factory suspension will change its geometry. This affects how the truck rides and handles. The changes can be mild or wild, depending on the amount of lift added and how it's done.

Body lifts and coil spring spacers keep the stock suspension and add a small boost. Body lifts add spacers between the body and the frame. Spring spacers add a polyurethane spacer on top of the coil springs to add a little height without affecting the factory suspension. Longer shocks are required with this style of lift kit. In addition, some vehicles require relocating or replacing the brake lines with longer ones.

These lifts are inexpensive and fairly easy to install. They will add 1 to 2 inches of extra room in the wheel wells for slightly larger tires.

Suspension lifts do much more. Longer coil springs and shocks allow more wheel travel up and down. This keeps the tires on the ground and

Articulation is the amount of tire movement up and down. It allows the vehicle to drive over uneven ground and keep the tires on the ground. In general, the more articulation the better. Solid axles will typically articulate better off-road than independent front suspension (IFS) axles. With solid axles, when one tire goes up, it puts pressure on the other tire by pushing down. With independent axles, each tire moves up and down without affecting the other tires. (Photo Courtesy Ogletree Photography/Shutterstock.com)

CHAPTER 9

Basic lift kits may increase the height of a truck or SUV but may lack the parts needed to correct the control arm or track bar geometry. This can affect the steering and handling of the truck. A true suspension system will include relocation brackets for brake lines and track bars. Longer front lower control arms will correct the caster, making the vehicle steer better. Look closely at the parts included in your kit and know what they do. Better yet, look for any extra parts that may be needed to correct the changes that a taller suspension may cause. (Photo Courtesy JKS Manufacturing)

provides better traction. In addition, having all four tires on the ground provides more stability and makes the vehicle feel less tippy.

The flexing of the suspension system is called articulation. As with many things in life, more is better. Suspension lifts range from basic kits with taller springs and shocks to proper suspension systems that not only lift the vehicle but also correct the steering geometry.

Leaf spring suspensions in older vehicles or on the rear axle of a pickup simply add more arch to the spring leafs to gain the additional height. Additional arch can cause a stiffer ride.

A proper coil spring suspension system often includes sturdy adjustable control arms. These will push the axles back into their factory position and maintain the original wheelbase. Brackets to relocate the track bars and brake lines will be included too. Adjustable track bars will allow you to center the axles left to right.

Having the axles centered and in their original positions help correct the steering and handling characteristics. They also allow adjustment needed to the caster for a good front-end alignment.

Taller suspension lifts may require longer driveshafts, and driveshaft vibration can occur due to the steep angle of the driveshafts and U-joints.

Wheels

Most people add taller suspensions to fit taller tires. Taller tires are usually wider too. This fact often requires an owner to buy wider wheels to accommodate the bigger tires. New wheels can dramatically improve the look of a truck.

Wheels and tires are the most common accessory purchase. Some people just want to change the look of their truck while others want to improve the ground clearance by increasing their tire size. Regardless of the motives, larger tires usually require wider wheels. The factory wheels are matched to the factory tire size. Wheel choices are almost infinite, so you should be able to find the wheels you like with the diameter, width, correct bolt pattern, and backspacing.

UPGRADES

Standard or Beadlock

There are several items to consider when buying new wheels. A good place to start is to consider whether standard wheels or beadlock wheels are needed.

For our purposes, standard wheels have a lip that is designed to fit the bead of the tire. Air pressure pushes the bead of the tire against the lip and prevents it from coming off.

Beadlock wheels clamp the bead of the tire, which prevents it from coming off regardless of the tire pressure. So, beadlock wheels can be used with less tire pressure.

However, there are compromises. While beadlock wheels are awesome, they cost more than standard aftermarket wheels and most are not DOT certified to be used on paved roads. When you see a set of beadlock wheels in use, they are often used with big tires on extremely difficult trails or in competition. Beadlock wheels require routine tightening of the beadlock rim bolts.

Bolt Pattern

The next thing to consider is the bolt pattern that the truck's axles have. Do you have five, six, or eight lug nuts? How far apart are the wheel studs. The new wheels should have the same bolt pattern as the truck.

While there are adapters and spacers available, they are a poor choice. Wheel adapters and spacers require routine tightening. They have been known to work loose or crack due to the stress on them. Buying wheels with the correct bolt pattern is always best.

Another consideration may be the size of the hole in the center of the wheel. If the truck has manual locking hubs, a bore size that allows the hubs to stick out through the hole is needed. This is usually an issue for older vehicles from the 1940s through 1980s.

If you have a newer model vehicle, be aware that its wheels may be hub-centric, which means that the aftermarket wheels need to be hub-centric as well. Hub-centric means that the wheel is centered by the center hub, not the lug nuts. Using the wrong style of wheel can cause vibration.

The width of the new tires will determine the width of the new wheel. When researching the tires

Standard wheels have a lip that uses air pressure to keep the tire bead in place. Low tire pressures may not hold the tire bead in place and can allow the tire to come off the wheel. Sharp turns at low tire pressure can also peel a tire off a wheel. Reseating the tire onto the wheel can be done by tightening a ratchet strap around the tread of the tire and adding air from an air compressor. (Photo Courtesy Method Race Wheels)

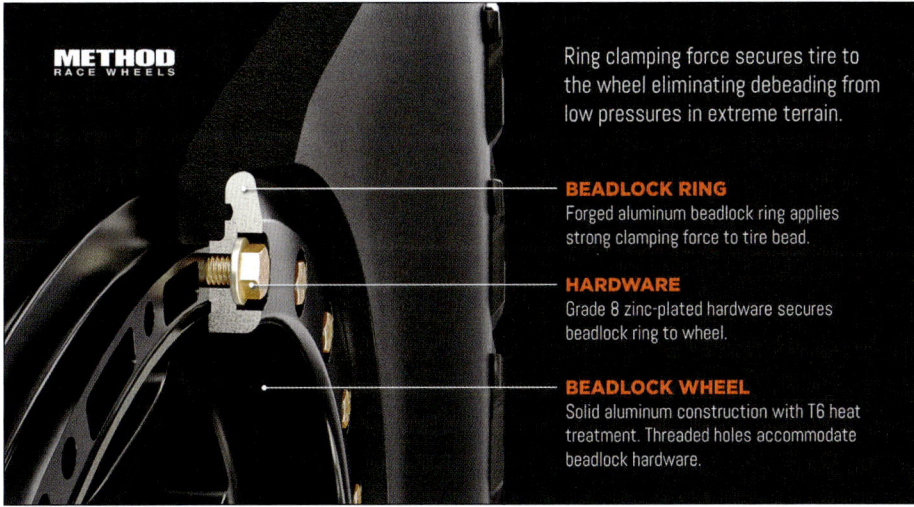

If you plan on driving off-road at low tire pressure on a regular basis, then buying beadlock wheels may be a good option. Just be aware that beadlock wheels may not be DOT legal for street use, they are usually more expensive, and they require routine maintenance. (Photo Courtesy Method Race Wheels)

CHAPTER 9

Larger diameter wheels have become more popular in recent years, but this causes the tire's sidewall to become shorter. This stiffens the ride on-road and allows less tire flex when aired down. Having a large tire on a small-diameter wheel provides better traction and a better ride off-road.

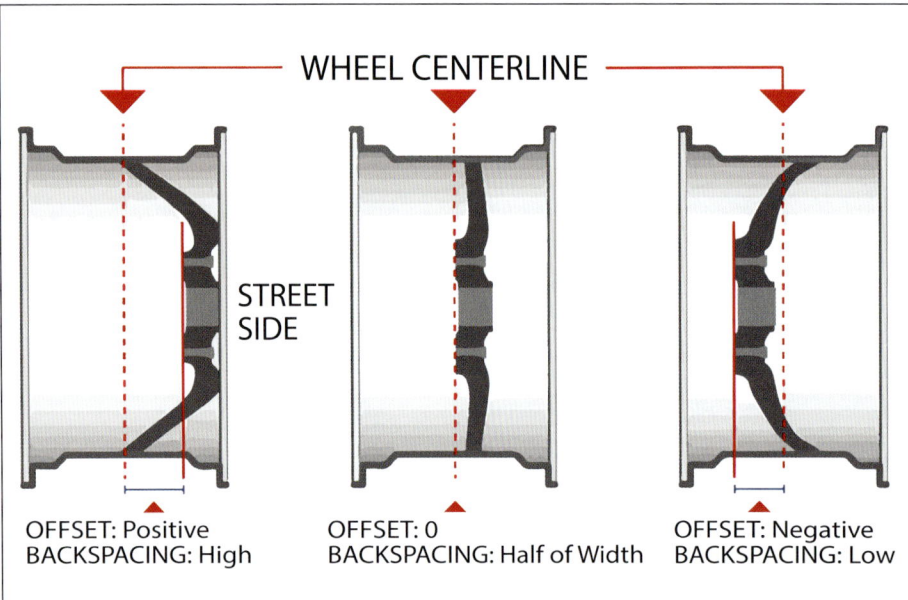

Backspacing measurements describe where the wheel's face is located within the wheel's rim. If the wheel face is closer to the mounting surface, the tires will stick out beyond the fender or fender flares. This allows the tires to spray mud and gravel up the side of the truck, and it's illegal in some states. Having the wheel face toward the outer lip of the wheel keeps more of the tire within the wheel well. However, in some cases, this can cause the front tires to rub on suspension components or the fender liner. It is best to test fit new wheels before they are mounted to the tires. Some tire shops have tools to test fit a wheel first.

that you want, the manufacturer will provide a range of approved wheel widths. Narrower wheels hold the tire bead better than wider wheels.

Most truck and SUV wheels range in diameter from 15 to 22 inches. The diameter of the new wheels will affect the height of the tire's sidewalls. Taller sidewalls allow more flex at lower tire pressures. Shorter sidewalls require higher tire pressure to keep the tire's bead on the wheel lip.

For example, a 35-inch tire on a 15-inch wheel will have 10-inch sidewalls. A 35-inch tire on a 22-inch wheel will only have 6.5-inch sidewalls. Taller sidewalls are better for off-road use. They allow the tire to flex and grip irregular surfaces, such as rocks and ledges.

Backspacing and Offset

The backspacing or offset of the new wheels is also important. Backspacing and offset describe where the wheel's mounting surface is located within the rim. This determines whether the wheel and tire are tucked under the fender flare or stick out.

Some states require that tires be covered by a fender flare and that they have mud flaps if the tires are not a stock size. The logic is that they want to prevent mud and gravel from flying off the tire onto the vehicle behind you.

Wheel backspacing is the measurement from the wheel's mounting surface to the outermost edge of the wheel. Backspacing is typically measured in inches. More backspacing means the wheels are pulled in under the fender. Less backspacing means the wheels are pushed out away from the body. This widens a vehicle's track and can put more pressure on the wheel bearings.

The offset of a wheel is the measurement from the wheel mounting surface to the center of the wheel. A wheel can have a zero, positive, or negative offset (measured in millimeters). A zero-offset wheel has the hub-mounting surface at the centerline of the wheel. A positive-offset wheel has the wheel-mounting surface positioned in the front half of the wheel, closer to the wheel face. Almost all aftermarket off-road wheels that are 9 inches wide or wider have a negative offset.

When adding wider wheels to a truck, keeping the factory offset becomes nearly impossible. For that reason, backspacing is the more important measurement. The amount of backspacing can also determine whether the new tires rub or if the front tires interfere with or limit the steering.

A good wheel and tire shop will know what size of wheels and tires that can safely be installed on your truck.

Tires

A tire's tread is its most important characteristic. The tire tread determines the amount of traction that a tire will have in a given condition. A snow tire's tread is very different than a mud tire's tread. Smooth street tires may perform well on dry pavement, but they are nearly worthless off-road.

The key to choosing a good tire tread is to be realistic about how the vehicle will be used. A 4x4 that is used for commuting and easier trail rides needs very different tread than an aggressive mud tire for a vehicle that is used in competition.

All-terrain tires have a tread with many grooves and sipes that allow

All-terrain tires are often a good choice for those who use their vehicles on the road most of the time. The grooves and siping also grip rocks, sand, or snow well when off-road. They have more tread on the ground than a mud tire. They are quieter than a mud tire, and they usually last longer too. All-terrain tires have the benefit of being a light truck (LT) tire with stronger sidewalls than a passenger car tire. (Photo Courtesy marekuliasz/Shutterstock.com)

them to grip well on wet roads, snowy roads, and sand. They have a lower noise level than mud tires and can last a long time if rotated as recommended. These tires are a good compromise for most people.

Many states in the snow belt will allow you to drive over mountain passes with tires that have a three-peak snowflake symbol on the sidewall. Without that type of tire, the state may require the use of snow chains.

If the trails are often muddy, then a mud tire may serve you better. The large lugs make more noise on the highway and wear out more rapidly, but they grip better on wet, muddy trails.

Nearly all modern tires are of a radial design. However, there are aggressive mud tires available that use a bias-ply design. These tires are

Some states that routinely receive snow have state laws about what tires are acceptable for winter driving. The three-peak snowflake logo on the sidewall makes it easy to determine if the tires comply with state snow laws. If the tires don't comply, snow chains will probably be required to get adequate traction. (Photo Courtesy YegoeVdo22/Shutterstock.com)

There are times when nothing but a mud tire will do. If you live where it rains a lot, the trails are going to be muddy. Dirt plus rain or snow equals mud. Modern radial mud-terrain tires are far better than they used to be, but they will still be louder than an all-terrain tire and will wear faster. They also do not stop on pavement as well because there is less tread contacting the road. (Photo Courtesy Vladimir Konstantinov/Shutterstock.com)

Every engineered system has a weak link. Ideally, the weak link should be something that is easy to reach and can be fixed on the trail. It would also be great if the weak link was cheap. Adding larger, heavier tires, lockers, and other accessories can add stress to the driveline and cause the weak link to break. U-joints, manual locking hubs, etc. can be replaced on the trail and are not too expensive. Breaking axle shafts, ring gears, and front unit bearings are more difficult and expensive to replace out on the trail. (Photo Courtesy Gary Yim/Shutterstock.com)

often used in competition events. Bias-ply tires have serious downsides when driven on the street. They develop flat spots when they sit, they are nearly impossible to balance, and they are loud and wear quickly on paved roads.

Larger tires can run lower tire pressure than stock-sized tires when supporting the same weight. Light truck tires can run lower tire pressure than passenger car tires due to their stiffer sidewalls.

Increasing the tire size affects several things. The bigger the tire, the greater the impact. Taller tires weigh more and will put more stress on wheel bearings and steering components and increase the braking distances. When tire size goes beyond the engineering limits for the axles, the axle shafts can break or the ring gear teeth inside the differential can be stripped. This can leave a driver stranded and cost a lot of money to replace. If the axle isn't upgraded, you will be replacing parts over and over again.

Keep in mind that installing taller tires will also change the number of revolutions that the tire travels per mile. This will confuse a vehicle's computer. The wheel sensors count

Tire Letters and Numbers

When reading tire sizes on the sidewall, there are a few things you need to know. Let's start by talking about a typical stock tire size. For example: 245/65R17.

The first number denotes the tire width in millimeters. The stock tire is 245 mm wide, which is equivalent to 9.6 inches.

The second number is the percentage of the width that makes up the sidewall of the tire. So, 65 percent of the 245 mm width is how tall the sidewall of the tire is. That comes out to be approximately 6.3 inches. Take that 6.3 inches and multiply it by 2 (since there is a sidewall both above and below the wheel) and then add the size of the wheel (17 inches) to get 29.6 inches, which is the approximate height of the tire.

The letter "R" stands for radial. The last number is the wheel diameter.

Date codes on tire sidewalls denote the age of the tire. The first two digits tell you the month, and the next two digits tell you the year. Most tire shops will not service a tire that is more than 10 years old. ∎

Since 2000, the week and year the tire was produced has been provided by the last four digits of the tire identification number with the two digits being used to identify the week immediately preceding the two digits used to identify the year. (Photo Courtesy Vladimir Razgulyaev/Shutterstock.com)

Most larger tire sizes are measured in inches. Most people want 33- to 40-inch-tall tires. The smaller tire sizes installed by the factory are usually in metric sizes. For example, if your current tire is a 245/65R17, this means that the tread is 245 mm wide (9.6 inches) with a sidewall that is 65 percent of that (6.3 inches). The "R" means that it is a radial-type tire, and the "17" means that the tire fits on a 17-inch wheel. A 245/65R17 tire is 29.6 inches tall (6.3-inch sidewall x 2 + 17-inch wheel diameter = 29.6 inches). (Photo Courtesy Vladimir Razgulyaev/Shutterstock.com)

CHAPTER 9

the revolutions and display that on the speedometer and odometer. Modern vehicles use wheel-sensor data for a variety of things from the ABS to traction control. The vehicle's computer needs to be adjusted to reflect the new tire size. A local car dealership can sometimes perform this task, or you can buy a programmer to adjust it yourself.

Programmers

Modern vehicles have computers that control a wide range of functions. When the tire diameter changes or the axles are regeared, it affects how the vehicle runs, shifts, and more. Aftermarket programmers compensate for the changes that are made so that the vehicle will run and drive normally. In addition, they can be set to override factory settings or display error codes. You can customize how your vehicle performs and disable annoying features that don't affect your safety.

Axles

Stock axles are designed and engineered for the tires they ship with from the factory. Some manufacturers build in a little margin of additional strength but not much. When the tire diameter is increased by more than 1 or 2 inches, you begin the descent down a slippery slope. This will exceed the capacity of the stock axles, and sooner or later parts will break.

This is where making the decision of how big to go is critical. Will 33- or 35-inch tires be enough, or do you want 37s or more?

Adding stronger axle shafts may solve one problem, but it will also create a new one. It is possible to replace broken axle shafts on the trail but not ring gears. You will keep finding weak points and spending money on fixing that only to move the weak point to somewhere else. In the end, more will be spent on repairs and upgrades than if the axles were replaced from the very beginning.

It's time to step back and consider how the vehicle will be used and what you bought. Did you buy the top-of-the-line Rubicon, TRD Pro, or Sasquatch? If so, do you really want to remove and replace the axles and lockers for which you paid extra?

If 40-inch tires were the goal from the beginning, it may be better to buy a basic vehicle and add custom axles from the start. That way, you can specify the axle gear ratios and lockers that you want. By the way, these custom axles will probably use eight-lug axle shafts, which means that those five- or six-lug wheels no longer fit.

Now comes the question of cost. Custom axles cost several thousand dollars. There may be modifications needed to the suspension, exhaust, and steering to install them. These are additional costs. In essence, you are redesigning and engineering the vehicle at this point.

It all comes back to figuring out what you want from the very beginning if you can.

More Upgrades

Adding larger tires changes the rolling diameter of the tire. This effectively changes the final gearing

It may be tempting to keep fixing the factory axles, but in the long run, it may be more cost effective to replace it completely with a stronger axle. (Photo Courtesy Rock Your 4x4)

110   THE ULTIMATE OFF-ROAD DRIVER'S GUIDE

UPGRADES

Tire Size versus Gear Ratio

Tire size (inches)	Gear ratio													
		3.07	3.21	3.31	3.42	3.55	3.73	3.91	4.11	4.27	4.56	4.88	5.13	5.29	5.38	5.71
	27	2483	2597	2677	2766	2872	3017	3163	3325	3454	3689	3947	4150	4279	4352	4619
	28	2395	2504	2582	2668	2769	2909	3050	3206	3331	3557	3806	4001	4126	4196	4540
	29	2312	2417	2493	2576	2674	2809	2945	3095	3216	3434	3675	3863	3984	4052	4300
	30	2235	2337	2410	2490	2584	2715	2846	2992	3109	3320	3553	3735	3851	3917	4157
	31	2163	2261	2332	2409	2501	2628	2755	2896	3008	3213	3438	3614	3727	3790	4023
	32	2095	2191	2259	2334	2423	2546	2669	2805	2914	3112	3331	3501	3610	3672	3897
	33	2032	2124	2191	2263	2349	2469	2588	2720	2826	3018	3230	3395	3501	3561	3779
	34	1972	2062	2126	2197	2280	2396	2512	2640	2743	2929	3135	3295	3398	3456	3668
	35	1916	2003	2065	2134	2215	2328	2440	2565	2664	2845	3045	3201	3301	3357	3563
	36	1862	1947	2008	2075	2154	2263	2372	2493	2598	2766	2961	3112	3209	3264	3464
	37	1812	1895	1954	2019	2095	2202	2308	2426	2520	2692	2881	3028	3123	3176	3370

- 🟨 Best gas mileage, poor performance
- 🟩 Good gas mileage, good performance
- 🟥 Poor gas mileage, best performance

It's fun and relatively easy to buy new wheels and taller tires. However, one thing to consider is that taller tires change the effective gear ratio in the axles. Small tire size increases may be okay with the factory gear ratio, but the bigger the tire size, the more dramatic the changes are in the performance of the truck or SUV. Acceleration will become sluggish, and the transmission will have to work harder. You may lose the ability to use top gear in some cases because the engine doesn't have the torque to propel these taller tires up hills.

that the truck experiences. Adding larger tires may make a truck feel sluggish as the engine, transmission, and axles struggle to turn the additional tire weight and diameter. The transmission may no longer use the top gear. Fuel economy will also decrease.

If you are buying a new vehicle, try to order the optional axle gear ratios. Opt for the lower ratios and save the time and money that regearing will cost later (4.10, 4.56, etc.). Regearing the differentials can be expensive, but it is usually worth it in the end. This is a job typically left to professionals. You only want to do this once, and it needs to be right.

Some folks who did not get locking differentials (lockers) when they bought their vehicle find that this is a good time to add them. There is a savings on labor once the axle is disassembled. In addition, if a little additional strength is desired for the axle shafts, they can be replaced with chrome-moly alloy axle shafts at the same time.

So, let's talk about replacing the ring and pinion gears to change the axle ratio. Lower gears compensate for the taller tires that were added. They restore the acceleration and torque that was lost.

Choosing the new gear ratio can be calculated by considering the difference in tire diameter between the old and new tires. Let's say the factory

Knowing the factory axle gear ratio is the first step to determine what gears are needed to return to the vehicle's stock performance. If buying a new vehicle and planning to install taller tires, consider the optional axle gear ratios when ordering. You could save a lot of money if you choose wisely.

31-inch tires were traded for 33-inch tires. That's roughly a 10-percent increase in diameter. A corresponding 10-percent decrease in gear ratio is needed to bring performance back to factory specifications.

Obviously, knowing the axle ratio that your vehicle already has is important. That information may be found on the window sticker or build sheet. If not, some axle manufacturers attach a metal tag to the differential cover bolts. The stock ratios usually range from 3.54 to 4.70.

If all else fails, spin one tire and count the number of turns on the rear driveshaft.

Open differentials allow the world to go round. Well, at least they allow the tires to turn in different arcs. This is especially true on paved roads where the driveline can bind up. (Photo Courtesy FotoDuets/Shutterstock.com)

1. Jack one rear wheel off the ground and set it on a jack stand. Put the transmission in neutral and disengage the parking brake.
2. Put a chalk mark on the tire and the driveshaft.
3. Turn the tire two revolutions and count the number of driveshaft turns. This process works for an open differential. If the vehicle has a limited-slip differential, only rotate the tire once.
4. The number of driveshaft rotations will tell you the axle ratio. For example, if the driveshaft turned four times, it's a 4.10:1 ratio.

So, let's say that your vehicle came with a 4.10 ratio and a 10-percent lower gear ratio is needed. Lower gear ratios are numerically higher. So, 4.10 x 1.1 = 4.51. The nearest ring and pinion axle ratio available is 4.56.

Lockers

Open differentials work well on paved roads and where traction is good, but as soon as things get slippery, their limitations become evident. If you've ever been stuck on wet grass, snow, or mud, you've probably experienced one tire spinning while the other tire is sitting still. In slippery conditions, all of the engine's torque is being applied to the one tire with the least amount of traction.

Open differentials were really designed for use on paved roads where the drivetrain can bind when going around corners. When turning, each of the four tires turns in a different arc, so each tire travels a different distance. The tires on the inside of the turn pivot, while the tires on the outside of the turn travel farther and faster to catch up.

Limited-slip differentials limit the amount of tire spin (slip) by applying some torque to each tire. One tire can still spin faster, but some of the power goes to the other tire. It is a compromise between an open differential and a locking differential. Limited-slip differentials work well on the street but still offer some additional traction in slippery conditions.

There are gear-driven limited-slip differentials and clutch-pack limited-slip differentials. Over time, the clutch packs can wear out, so the gear-driven style is favored.

Locking differentials provide the most traction. There are two basic styles: automatic and selectable. The automatic style of locker works all the time. Once it is installed, there is no ability to turn it on or off. This means that when making turns on paved roads the tires will spin at the same speed because they are "locked" together. This can cause chirping of the tires, internal clunking noises, and unusual handling quirks. This is especially true with short-wheelbase vehicles. In a turn, one tire pivots while the other one is forced to catch up.

Selectable lockers can be turned on and off as needed. This is the best

UPGRADES

Locking differentials should only be used when needed. This saves wear and tear on the drivetrain and prevents unwanted handling quirks.

There will always be weak parts in the drivetrain. Think about the modifications being made and what this will affect. What is the easiest part to fix or replace on the trail if something breaks? Broken ring gears or axle shafts can be difficult to replace on the trail. U-joints are easier. (Photo Courtesy Shyam Patel)

Sturdy winch bumpers are a wonderful upgrade over stock plastic bumpers. However, look at the design carefully and make sure that the winch that you want will fit. It's very important to be able to see and move the winch line when respooling it. (Photo Courtesy Warn Industries)

solution for street-driven vehicles. It acts as an open differential on the street with none of the handling quirks and acts as a full locking differential when activated off-road. It is the best of both worlds.

As you can imagine, using lockers puts additional strain on the axle's differential when engaged, so they need to be used carefully. They should be engaged before you get stuck and turned off after you are past the obstacle that required them. There are times when it's best to not use lockers, such as in slippery conditions on an off-camber trail or when using lockers will auger or corkscrew you to the low side. Some manufacturers use selectable lockers in their top-of-the-line models.

It is still possible to get stuck when using lockers, but they can be a helpful tool. They are not magic and shouldn't be used as a crutch.

Axles

Larger tires add additional strain on all of the axle parts, including the axle shafts. If a stock axle shaft breaks, it is probably time to upgrade to chrome-moly axle shafts. There are various alloys available. Stronger front axle shafts will probably change the weak point to the U-joints. U-joints are easier to replace on the trail than axle shafts. However, be aware that something has to give, and it may be the teeth on the ring gear. There are no heavy-duty ring and pinion sets available. When they break, it means rebuilding the differential and possibly replacing the locker.

Front Winch Bumpers

Sooner or later, you may decide that having an electric winch would be a good idea. When all else fails, a quality winch will usually get a vehicle unstuck. However, that winch needs to have a sturdy mount to withstand the pulling force that the winch produces.

Most modern 4WD vehicles are delivered with plastic and foam bumpers to save weight and meet federal requirements for fuel economy and impact resistance. While this is understandable, these bumpers are not sturdy enough to mount an electric winch.

The number of winch-ready steel front bumpers that are available for most 4WD vehicles is amazing, especially for the most popular 4WD models. They come in all shapes, sizes, and finishes. While most are sturdy enough for the job, there is an almost infinite number of styles available. It can be hard to choose.

When choosing a front bumper, verify that it bolts directly to the vehicle's frame or subframe. The winch will put a few tons of pulling force on the bumper, and it needs to be well mounted.

Other things to consider are whether the bumper has strong tow points. These are necessary when recovering a stuck vehicle. Some bumpers have provisions for factory or aftermarket fog lights. Ideally, the bumper is designed to mount the winch low in the bumper so that the winch doesn't block much airflow to the radiator. It's critical to be able to see and reach the winch cable or rope once the winch is in place. Hidden or semi-hidden winch bumpers make it difficult to access the winch controls and to respool the winch cable or rope after its use.

Look for a truck that is similar to yours with the bumper that you want installed. A 4WD retail shop may have some on display. Another option is to check 4WD trail rides or events for other drivers who have the bumper(s) that you're considering. The bumper, winch plate, and winch are a sizable purchase, so you want to be sure that it meets your needs.

Adding a winch bumper, winch plate, and a winch are smart upgrades. They can make the difference between driving or walking home. However, they are usually expensive; do your research so that you have no regrets. (Photo Courtesy 4Wheel Parts)

Winch Plates and Winches

Winch plates are simply a sturdy steel plate that bolts to the vehicle's frame or subframe. Then, a winch can be bolted to it. Virtually all electric winches use the same bolt pattern with four bottom-mounted bolts that have a 4.5-inch by 10-inch pattern.

Winches are an amazing tool when used safely. They can also be dangerous if they are used by an uneducated owner. If buying a winch, take a 4WD class to learn how to use it safely. It will be well worth the cost and will keep your fingers intact.

Winches come in all levels of strength and price points. The first thing to determine is how much pull is needed for your vehicle. The general rule of thumb is to take the weight of the vehicle and buy a winch with 1.5 times that weight. So, if you have a 5,000-pound pickup truck, get a 7,500-pound winch. The nearest size that you are likely to find is an 8,000-pound winch.

Winch ratings are measured when nearly all of the winch line has been pulled out. They have the most pulling power on the bottom layer. While long winch lines may make sense if there aren't many trees in your area, it also means that a lot of line has to be used to get the maximum pulling strength. One solution is to carry a winch line extension for extra reach.

The next consideration is whether a steel cable or a synthetic rope is best for the winch line. There are advantages and disadvantages for both.

UPGRADES

Virtually all modern electric winches use the same bolt pattern underneath: 4.5 inches x 10 inches. The key is to be sure that the winch plate fits your vehicle and that it is sturdy. It will be under a lot of strain. It must bolt to the vehicle's frame or subframe. (Photo Courtesy Warn Industries)

A quality winch is priceless when you need it. This is one item that you don't want to fail. Training on how to use it safely is important. You'll be amazed at what a winch can do if used properly. (Photo Courtesy Warn Industries)

The cable can also tangle among the layers on a winch drum. Steel cables like to lay flat. When wound tightly on a winch drum, they have a lot of tension. They also tend to have broken strands that create burrs or splinters that can catch on a glove and pull it off. They will hurt your hands if handled barehanded. Never handle any winch line without gloves.

A winch with a steel cable will cost less than the same winch with a synthetic rope. Steel cables often weigh about 17 pounds, while a synthetic rope of equal size will weigh less than 3 pounds. Steel cables are very resistant to abrasion. If you are winching in rocky areas on a regular basis, they will probably last longer than a rope. However, steel cables will crush or twist if wound onto a winch drum improperly.

Lastly, steel cables store more energy due to their weight. If the cable breaks, it will whip back and forth. It can seriously hurt or kill anyone standing in its path.

Synthetic ropes used for winches can cost more than double that of a steel cable. However, they have many safety advantages and are actually stronger than a steel cable of an equal size.

Winch ropes have no memory, so they will wrap around a winch drum with no tension. They are also much easier to pull out when needed. They are safer due to their light weight. They will still whip

Everything has a downside, and for steel winch cables it is that they tend to break strands when wrapped tightly around a winch drum. The broken strands can snag on a glove as the cable is handled. (Photo Courtesy chadum888/Shutterstock.com)

THE ULTIMATE OFF-ROAD DRIVER'S GUIDE

CHAPTER 9

The bottom layers of winch cable can crush or twist under tension if not respooled neatly. In addition, the cable can become wedged between layers if it is not properly spooled.

If a winch will be used more than a few times each year, upgrade to a synthetic winch line. They are lighter and easier to unspool when needed. They are also safer in the rare event that it breaks. However, they are more expensive. Luckily, it's fairly easy to change from steel cable to synthetic line. (Photo Courtesy Warn Industries)

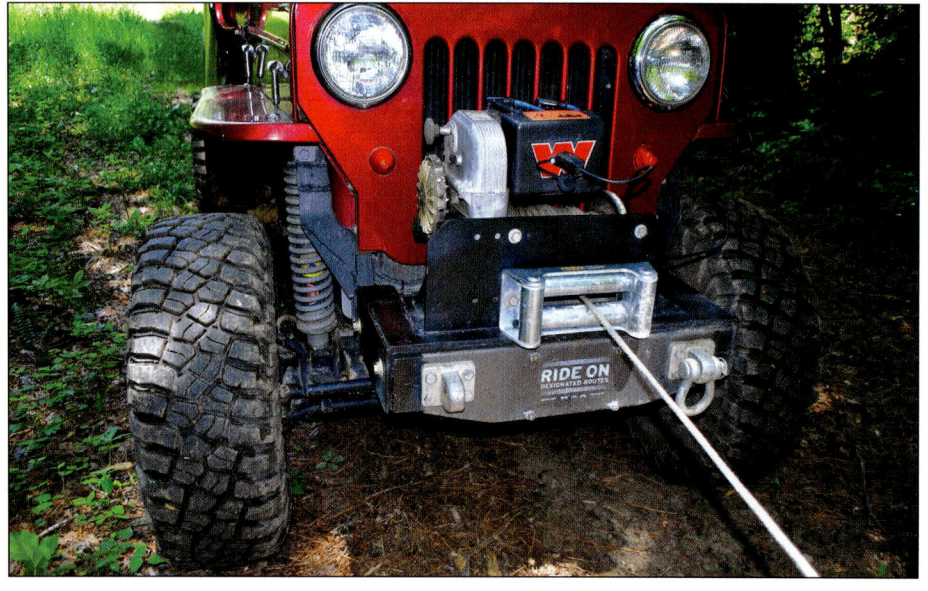

Virtually all winch manufacturers ship hawse fairleads with their synthetic line winches. They are lighter and cheaper to manufacture. However, the synthetic winch line rubs across the aluminum fairlead, which creates friction and heat. That heat can weaken the line or remove a little bit of rope material. Roller fairleads allow the steel cable or synthetic rope to pass along the roller without creating friction.

if they break but with much less force. Also, they can be tied in a knot or spliced to be used again and again.

Synthetic ropes are more vulnerable to abrasion and will fray if pulled across an obstacle. Many manufacturers will include a chaff guard to protect the rope in these situations. Ropes can also degrade from UV exposure if left outdoors for long periods. Ropes will fade if left outdoors, and at some point, they will become brittle.

Roller fairleads are usually shipped with steel cable winches. When the cable rubs against a roller fairlead, the roller spins. It's pretty common for winch manufacturers that sell winches with synthetic line to include an aluminum hawse fairlead. The problem with these fairleads is that when a synthetic line rubs against it, friction is created and that can degrade the line.

Roller fairleads work best with both winch cables and lines.

Skid Plates

Skid plates are usually included by manufacturers on 4WD trucks and SUVs with an off-road package. They are fine for light use on gravel roads and soft terrain, such as sand, snow, or mud. However, if you plan to drive on trails with rocks, replace the factory offerings with sturdy, full-coverage skid plates.

Steel or aluminum skid plates protect the vital drivetrain components that are vulnerable to damage. Quality skid plates are usually made from 3/16-inch material. Heavier vehicles need thicker skid plates. A four-door SUV may need 1/4-inch-thick material.

While skid plates are not sexy, they are less expensive than replacing a transmission, transfer case, or gas tank. No matter what size lift or tires are installed, you will continue to contact rocks from time to time.

Rock Sliders versus Steps

Straddling rocks or logs can result in damage or getting stuck.

No matter how much a vehicle is lifted, it will still occasionally hit obstacles. That can cause expensive damage or even leave a driver stranded. While skid plates aren't usually seen, they provide great protection and peace of mind. (Photo Courtesy Warn Industries)

One way to get over an obstacle is to put a front tire on it to lift your truck up and over it. The problem is that when the tire rolls forward, the rock or log will contact the rocker panel and drag along it until the rear tire arrives to lift the truck again. Rocker

There is a big difference between side steps and rock sliders. Side steps are a convenient way to get in and out of a truck or SUV easier. They work great, but they usually won't support the weight of the truck. (Photo Courtesy nyker/Shutterstock.com)

CHAPTER 9

Rock sliders protect the rocker panel when driving over rocks or logs. They need to be made of thick metal and be mounted to the vehicle's frame or subframe. If the truck or SUV has a lot of lift, consider rock sliders with a powered step that drops out the bottom of the slider.

Factory support structures improve with each new model to meet stricter safety standards. However, they are designed for one-time use in the event of a rollover accident. A true roll cage is designed for racing or high-risk driving. A good roll cage will last the lifetime of the vehicle.

panels are low hanging and vulnerable to damage.

Most manufacturers are now offering plastic steps to reduce weight and cost. These bend or break at the first contact with a rock or a log. Side steps aren't much better. They were never designed to support the weight of a vehicle, so they bend or crush on impact.

True rock sliders stretch from the front fender to the rear fender and are strong enough to support the weight of the vehicle while it slides over the obstacle. They are usually tucked up high to provide as much ground clearance as possible. Fixing body damage is expensive, and when you're done, you still have the same vulnerability. Rocky trails demand protection for the undercarriage and the body.

Roll Cages

Auto manufacturers are making vehicles that are safer and safer. Most of those efforts are focused on electronic features. Automatic emergency braking, adaptive cruise control, blind-spot monitoring, lane departure, and cross-traffic detection are just a few of the safety features that are being added. However, these features are focused on highway use, not off-road adventures.

With that being said, the body and inner structure of new vehicles are getting better too. Liability concerns prevent auto manufacturers from calling a roll bar a "roll bar," but Jeep's "Sport Bar" is stronger than ever.

Keep in mind that the Sport Bar is not designed for serious competition events or extreme trails, where rolling over is a real possibility. Only you can decide if your use will require a stronger solution. There are aftermarket companies that make sport bar accessories to strengthen the factory offering, and there are companies that also make a full-replacement roll cage for serious off-road use.

LEDs

The evolution of automotive lighting has been slow. We've gone from flickering gas lamps to Halogen bulbs over the course of 100 years. In general, light-emitting diodes (LEDs) have been a major step forward. Initially, auto manufacturers offered them as an option, and the aftermarket began selling them as an accessory. LED headlights and fog lights have greatly improved safety.

LED lightbars, however, are illegal for use on-road. Some states require that lightbars be covered when a vehicle is driven on-road. They are restricted to off-road use only. While they are bright, they can easily blind other off-road drivers. Basically, you have to be alone off-road for them to be of practical use. However, in those situations, they are a powerful tool.

LEDs draw very little electricity and may flicker with the pulses of 12-volt DC power. The frequency of the pulses may not match that of the vehicle's computer. This is usually seen in LED headlights and can be solved with anti-flicker adapters.

LEDs do not produce heat like Halogen headlights. This causes

UPGRADES

Adding wider fender flares will solve the incorrect backspacing problem if they are available for your truck or SUV. (Photo Courtesy Bushwacker/Truck Hero)

When replacing factory wheels and tires, it is common to have the incorrect backspacing. This causes the tires to stick out beyond the fenders or fender flares. This will cause gravel and mud to spray up the side of the truck or out behind you. This is illegal in some states.

issues when the weather is cold. The lenses on LED lights can freeze over, blocking their light. A few high-quality LED headlight producers offer versions with a heating grid to melt the accumulating ice. LED lightbars typically have cooling fins. The fins are known to cause whistling at highway speeds.

In most states, it is illegal to display blue or red lights, especially if they flash or strobe. Those colors are reserved for the police and fire departments. Headlight halos, rock lights, and others need to be any color other than blue or red. The logic behind this is that your vehicle should not be confused with a law enforcement or emergency vehicle.

Fender Flares

When adding bigger tires, it is fairly common for the tires to extend out beyond the factory fender flares, especially if the wheel backspacing is off. This is illegal in some states due to the windshield damage caused by flying gravel to following vehicles. There are many rural areas in America with gravel roads, and flying gravel is an issue.

In addition, mud can cover the side of the truck or SUV. That may sound okay until you have to open the door or roll down a window. Then, it becomes a muddy mess. There are several aftermarket companies that make wider fender flares.

Interior Protection

Speaking of a muddy mess, on any given trail ride, some of the outdoors is going to join you on the interior of your vehicle. A wide variety of products are available to protect the cargo area, seats, and floors.

Rooftop Tents and Skottles

Many people go out for one-day trail rides, especially in the Eastern United States. Recently, there is a growing trend where people want to travel greater distances and camp overnight. Backcountry travel is an idea that has been around for a long time. Beginning in the 1920s, people would outfit their cars and go camping in national parks. Some would take their families and travel all summer.

As you can imagine, the equipment has gotten better over the last 100 years. Now, a driver can take a well-designed new vehicle and spend thousands of dollars adding a lot of weight by installing roof racks, rooftop tents, sliding kitchens, 12-volt refrigerators, and skottles. Solar panels and dual battery systems are common. You'll want to keep additional weight as low as possible. Top-heavy vehicles become tippy.

There is too much backcountry camping equipment to describe here. There are endless choices, but

CHAPTER 9

Roughly half of Americans are overweight, and their vehicles are too. Luckily, it's easy to sort through your gear to decide what's really necessary versus what's nice to have along.

Backcountry camping has been around for a long time. This is what most Americans still do today. True overlanding usually involves foreign vehicle–based travel for extended periods to see new places and enjoy different cultures.

always choose quality items. No one wants to buy something twice. If it's cheap, flip it over and look for the country of origin. That can give you a hint about the quality. Be sure to ask others who have the same goals as you. My advice is to go simple at first while you learn what you like and want.

Learn what the vehicle's total weight capacity is. Add up the total weight of you and all passengers, the vehicle (curb weight), and all of the equipment. Then, look up the vehicle's gross vehicle weight rating (GVWR). That weight rating can usually be found on a decal in the driver's doorjamb. If not, look it up in the owner's manual or online.

For example: the curb weight of a 2021 four-door Jeep Wrangler Rubicon is 4,449 pounds. It has a maximum payload of 892 pounds, including passengers. Let's say that you and your one passenger together weigh 300 pounds. That means that you can only add 592 pounds of stuff before you hit the maximum weight that the engineers designed the vehicle to carry.

It's a really good idea to weigh your vehicle at a truck stop before making modifications. This tells you about the actual weight before adding accessories and gear. Weigh the vehicle again when it is ready for the trail. Have a full tank of gas, the typical passengers, and all the trail gear. This weight will determine if you are under or over the GVWR.

Trading plastic bumpers for steel ones adds weight. Adding a winch and winch plate adds weight, larger tires add weight, and so on. It adds up quickly. Some aftermarket companies now offer aluminum bumpers and skid plates to help reduce weight. Using a synthetic winch rope saves about 15 pounds over a steel cable.

Exceeding the GVWR can cause poor braking, a sagging suspension, and faster wear on many components. It can dramatically change the quality and safety of your ride. So, weigh all of the options carefully.

Your 4WD truck or SUV was engineered to meet but not exceed the gross vehicle weight rating (GVWR). This is the combined weight of the vehicle, fuel, passengers, and gear. If your vehicle is heavier than this, it can affect the way the vehicle handles, stops, and steers. If the weight is on the roof of the vehicle, it will sway more and be tippy. It can take much longer to stop. In addition, the tall, soft tires will be slower to respond to steering wheel movements. Additional weight also puts more strain on the bearings, bushings, and other components. Knowing your "before" and "after" weight can help identify problems before they happen. (Photo Courtesy Marina-foodblogger/Shutterstock.com)

CHAPTER 10

TRAIL REPAIRS

Please keep in mind that we are focusing on trail repairs, not maintenance. Preventive maintenance should be done at home or in a professional shop before an off-road trip.

Trail repairs happen when something breaks and prevents you from driving to the nearest road or town safely. Trail repairs are temporary and intended for slow-speed driving to "get out." They are not meant to be driven on the interstate at high speeds for hours.

Diagnosing that funny noise should be done sooner rather than later. Mechanical things seldom heal themselves. Finding and fixing a problem early can be easier than dealing with the disaster when a critical part falls off. In time, you will learn which noises are normal for your vehicle and which are not.

Some problems are really easy to find, but some are more subtle. When something doesn't feel or sound right, tell others in the group over the radio and try to find a wide, flat, dry spot to pull over. Don't block the trail for others.

Then, start looking around for the source of the problem. A gallery of well-intentioned people will probably be standing around watching you and offering free advice. Occasionally, someone will be along who has experienced the same problem in the past.

If the problem is found, try to figure out how long it will take to fix it and let the trail leader know if you are traveling in a group. The trail leader can then decide whether to have the whole group wait while you make the repair or to leave the tail gunner with you and move on.

If the repair can be made within 15 minutes or so, keep the group together. If it seems like it will take longer, the leader may decide to continue the trail ride so as to not delay everyone's plans. There are few

It is not unusual to hear squeaks and groans under a truck as the suspension moves up and down. Rattles may indicate that something is loose, but it could be something moving around inside the cargo area too. Loud snaps or cracks may mean that a driveline part is broken. Squealing noises are probably coming from the skid plates as they scrape over the rocks. You will eventually be able to identify what noises are "normal" and which need to be investigated.

THE ULTIMATE OFF-ROAD DRIVER'S GUIDE

CHAPTER 10

Tightening a loose nut may be a quick repair, but others will take longer. Take your time when diagnosing the problem so that you get it right. Once you know what needs to be fixed, let the trail leader know so that he or she can decide whether to wait or to move on.

Check engine lights can come on for a variety of reasons. Some may indicate the need for urgent repairs and others do not. Some solutions are as easy as tightening the gas cap until it clicks (P0455 and/or P0457). However, only a code scanner will really tell you which codes are being shown. Most often, the codes only give you vague general information. It's a place to start a diagnosis, but it may not be specific enough. If the vehicle starts, stops, steers, and drives okay, keep going but have it checked out soon at a dealership or repair shop. Code scanners can be found at auto parts stores if you want your own. (Photo Courtesy virgmos/Shutterstock.com)

things as motivational as watching a line of vehicles drive off, leaving you with one or two helpers to fix a problem.

Modern 4WD trucks and SUVs tend to be well built and reliable. When they do have an issue, it is usually electronic. For example, a sensor may not transmit or receive signals properly with the computer. Most sensors are pretty rugged, but they do get bounced around a lot and may get wet or muddy.

When the check engine light comes on, it usually does not require a trail repair or towing. However, if the light starts blinking, pull over immediately and investigate as soon as it's safe to do it. Check the fluid levels and look under the hood for anything that looks out of place. Shut the vehicle off, wait a short time, and then restart the vehicle. This may reset the computer. If not, disconnect the primary battery for 15 minutes to clear the error codes and reset the check engine light.

If the truck or SUV seems to be running and driving normally, you can probably continue on the trail ride. However, you should have the error codes read by a shop or dealership when you are back in town.

In an ever-changing effort to make new vehicles more idiot-resistant and autonomous, there are certain driver actions that can cause electronic issues. Applying the gas pedal and brake pedal at the same time, may cause the check engine light to come on. The computer is trying to prevent unintended acceleration.

In some vehicles, if you press the brake pedal and put the transmission in drive with the door open, the vehicle will not move. The transmission will stay in park until the door is closed. These features may be irritating,

TRAIL REPAIRS

Older vehicles tend to be simpler (with fewer electronics) but with higher maintenance. Owner's manuals from the past told you to adjust the valves to a specified gap. Gapping the points was necessary before electronic ignitions. It was common for people to have a timing light and dwell meter in their home garage. Today, all of this is done "automagically." It's great when it works, but it can be a mystery when it doesn't.

In time, you will learn your truck or SUV's weaknesses. Cleaning and inspecting everything under the truck after a trail adventure will help you find and fix weak or broken parts before the next trip. Look for shiny parts that have been rubbing on something. Look for bent, dented, or missing parts. Grab and wiggle parts to see if they are loose. These are usually the suspension, driveshafts, and steering components. Wipe the mud and grease off the zerk fittings and pump some grease into them. A dry ball joint, tie-rod end, or U-joint will fail. (Photo Courtesy Rock Your 4x4)

but they won't prevent you from driving home.

Anyone who owns a vehicle with the dual battery AutoStart feature will need to learn how to jump-start the vehicle using the starting battery as opposed to the accessory battery. It is important to learn the proper jump-start procedure because you can easily melt the fuse panel under the hood if you get it wrong. Modern CAN bus electrical systems are far more sensitive to voltage than the old wiring systems.

Older vehicles are far simpler, but the original parts may be older than the driver, and the modified parts or accessories see a lot of stress. Maintenance is important on all 4WD vehicles, but even more so on older trucks. Older vehicles may have 20 or more greaseable zerk fittings on the driveline, suspension, and steering components, while newer vehicles may have sealed U-joints, tie-rod ends, etc.

If you have a newer vehicle that is not highly modified, all you may need are some basic tools to tighten any fasteners that come loose. If you are driving a highly modified older vehicle on huge tires with lots of power, more spare parts and tools need to be brought and your mechanical knowledge needs to be good.

Fitment

Carrying the correct spare parts with you is a good idea. However, there are limits. You can't carry everything that might fail. Instead, do some research to see what parts commonly fail on the make and model of your vehicle when driven off-road. These are the weak links.

Carrying the tools that are needed to replace those parts can mean the difference between walking and driving to the nearest paved road.

We sometimes joke that when a part breaks, it's an opportunity to upgrade. However, think it through. Replacing stock parts with stronger parts may seem like a good idea but may actually just create a new weak link. Think about which part is likely to break next if it is overstressed. Replacing a broken ring gear inside the axle's differential is not a typical trail repair.

Does this mean that you shouldn't upgrade parts? No, it means that you need to carefully research the effects of your upgrades. You may want to replace a weak-link part at home so that you know how to do it on the trail. Take notes on the tools that were used and the part numbers. It's far easier to learn at home on a garage floor or driveway than while lying on a snowy or muddy trail.

Kits

The tools needed to replace a U-joint or axle shaft can be put in a separate container or kit so that everything needed is in one place.

Electrical

Some people carry an electrical kit that contains spare fuses, a bit of

CHAPTER 10

extra wire, butt connectors, electrical tape, and electronic contact drying spray. Having a wire cutting and stripping tool is helpful. A voltmeter can be really helpful too.

U-Joint

A U-joint kit might include the spare U-joints, a C-clamp, a small grease gun, and the correct-size hand tools. Spare U-joints straps, C-clips, and even a spare cap or yoke may be helpful, depending on the vehicle.

Tire Repair

A tire repair kit should include a high-quality tire plug kit and extra valve stems. A tire valve-stem puller makes replacement of a damaged valve stem much easier. A tire crayon allows you to mark the location of the puncture. A ratchet strap can be applied to the circumference of the tire to push out the sidewalls. This can reseat a tire bead if the tire separates from the wheel due to low tire pressure.

Fluids

Having extra fluids can be helpful, but you usually don't need a huge amount. Bring a few quarts of oil, some coolant, gear oil for the axles, and transmission fluid if you have an automatic transmission. Add some brake fluid and power-steering fluid too. A critical tool can be a small plastic fluid pump for use with the gear oil. A funnel can be pretty helpful too.

Tarp

A cheap plastic tarp to throw on the ground under the truck before starting repairs can keep you dry. A magnetic parts tray can prevent you from losing small parts as you remove and then reinstall them.

Cleaning

When you are done with a repair, you will most likely have greasy hands. Hand cleaner and some shop towels or rags can be a blessing. Some people prefer to wear nitrile gloves when working on their truck. The gloves keep the grease off your hands and can be thrown away when you get home.

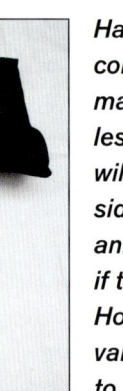

Having a kit for common part repairs makes the repair less frustrating and will save time. Trailside repairs can be annoying, especially if the weather is bad. However, there is value in not having to drag everything out of the vehicle to rummage for the right parts and tools. Waterproof boxes in bright colors keep a kit together and the contents dry. Get one slightly larger than needed so that tools can be added in the future.

Having a cheap plastic tarp or shower curtain liner can seem like a miracle when making a repair on a wet, muddy, or snowy trail. They fold up flat and take up very little space. However, they will be a mess after the repair, so also carry a few heavy-duty construction trash bags. A magnetic tray (or two) allows you to keep critical small parts in one place. It's really easy to lose parts when working on the ground.

Adapt and Overcome

You'll need to assess what's not working and figure out how to compensate. Here are some common examples:

- If the rear driveshaft breaks, remove it and drive out in 4WD low range using the front driveshaft. You may need help over obstacles from others in your group. Tow the truck or SUV home once it reaches pavement. Make sure that you have sufficient fluid in the transfer case. Some transfer cases have a slip yoke that leaks gear oil when the rear driveshaft is removed.
- If the front driveshaft fails, remove it, and drive out in 4WD low range using the rear driveshaft. Shift into 2WD high range when you reach a paved road, and you'll be fine for the drive home.
- If you bend the tie-rod or drag link, gently try to pull it straight with a winch. Then remove the tie-rod end and slide a Hi-Lift jack handle over the tie-rod or draglink for strength. Be sure to count the number of turns that it took to remove the tie-rod end and then thread it back in the same number of turns. This will keep the steering alignment about the same.
- If the steering linkage is broken, a vehicle can be slowly towed out backward. The front wheels will follow along, but turns may require some help. Having fellow drivers push the tires in the desired direction can make turns easier.
- A broken brake line can sometimes be pinched off with a pair of locking pliers. The remaining three brakes will work. Be sure to refill the brake master cylinder with DOT 3 brake fluid.

Broken or bent parts can be held up or out of the way with ratchet straps, cable ties (zip ties), or mechanic's wire (bailing wire). These items can also be used to hold parts together.

People have made some impressive temporary repairs with these items. Ingenuity is key. However, so is safety. No one wants to end up in an internet video because something failed.

Critical Thinking

Critical thinking skills are a big help. Understanding the problem and figuring out how to fix it with what you have can be scary or rewarding, depending on your perspective. Some drivers relish the challenge while others want to put a for sale sign on the truck and walk away.

Trail Repairs

Most trail repairs are simple. By far the most common trail repair has to do with tires. Modern tires are far better than before. Stronger sidewalls make a big difference. When air is let out of a tire at the trailhead to air down, the sidewalls bulge. This makes them more vulnerable to cuts and punctures.

Tires take the brunt of the punishment because they are in contact with the trail. Punctures can be easily plugged with a quality tire repair kit with sturdy metal reaming and plugging tools. Sidewall cuts can also be fixed, if necessary, but it may be easier to install the spare tire before going to this much effort. If you are riding with similar vehicles to yours, you may be able to borrow someone else's spare tire if needed.

When all else fails, a cut sidewall can be repaired. Once the damaged tire is off the vehicle, drill or cut small holes along the edges of the cut and then stitch the cut closed with the metal wire that is included in the tire repair kit. This is unlikely to seal the tire, but any gaps can be filled with tire plugs. Success with this technique may vary.

Carrying an inner tube may be a good idea if you are driving in areas that have sharp rocks. However, installing an inner tube can be a lot of work. It requires deflating the tire and separating the tire bead from the wheel. Standing or jumping on the tire's sidewall may work, or you can use a Hi-Lift jack to press down on the sidewall.

The wheel's valve stem also needs to be removed. Then, slide the inner tube inside the tire and push its valve stem through the valve-stem hole in the wheel. Be sure that there are no sharp edges or steel belts on the inside of the tire that could damage the inner tube. Then, reinflate the inner tube. This repair is only for emergency trail use. It will not get you home. The tire needs to be replaced.

If the spare tire is badly damaged and you have a second flat tire, try a tire plug. If that fails, an inner tube is the last resort.

OEM engineers design vehicles to be reliable when driven in stock condition. They build safe, efficient

CHAPTER 10

Once you wear the "new" off a 4WD truck or SUV, maintenance begins. Hoses and seals may begin to leak. It's best to replace these items at home, but you may be surprised one day on the trail when something requires a repair. Making a temporary trail repair may get you home so it can be fixed properly later.

vehicles that meet federal standards and can be warranted. However, enthusiasts take these vehicles and modify them for our purposes. We want to make them more capable off-road, but the necessary upgrades can cause other issues.

The additional weight of larger wheels and tires add stress to driveline parts. The brakes become less effective, and the driveshaft and axle U-joints can fail. If your truck or SUV has an independent front suspension (IFS) the constant velocity (CV) joints may be overwhelmed and break. Wheel bearings wear faster and so do the ball joints, tie-rod ends, and more. Even the grease becomes contaminated by water and mud.

The power-steering system was designed for tires up to 33 inches, but we roll out the credit card and have 40-inch tires installed. Naturally, this causes a domino effect.

So, plan accordingly, upgrade where appropriate, and carry spare parts. It is unlikely that someone else on the trail will have the exact parts you need. The local auto parts store probably doesn't have them either. In fact, even the aftermarket manufacturer who made your heavy-duty parts might be temporarily out of stock when you call.

Are You Dripping?

Another common trail fix involves leaking fluids. Hoses fail or the hose clamps loosen. Carrying spare coolant and heater hoses, hose clamps, and fluids is a good idea on older vehicles. There are a variety of products designed to stop leaks. They can make good temporary repairs.

A few oil drips are common, but if the oil pan or automatic transmission pan is punctured, you'll need something to fix it. In this situation, drain the oil, remove the oil pan, and beat it back into its original shape with a small drill hammer. Then, apply JB Weld or a similar sealant to fill the gap in the crack. Once the sealant has dried, reinstall the oil pan and refill the engine or transmission with oil. A catch pan or heavy-duty trash bag are needed to capture most of the oil being drained and then poured back into the engine or transmission. A funnel may be a good idea.

Top off the oil level with the spare fluids you carry. Borrow oil or transmission fluid from other drivers if needed. A fluid spill kit is also a big help. These kits may be required on some trails. We don't want to pollute the local streams or rivers.

Stubborn Parts

Suspension bolts experience tremendous stress. It is a good idea to carry a few extra nuts and bolts as well as the tools needed to install them. Most metric hand tool sets only go up to 19 mm. These large suspension bolts and nuts may be 21 mm or larger. Having a 1/2-inch breaker bar and socket can provide the leverage needed to remove or tighten the nut. A dab of thread locker can keep the nuts tight when you're done.

A spray can of penetrating fluid can be useful too. PB B'laster, WD-40, and similar products are widely available. Soak the threaded end of the bolt and nut and let the fluid work for a little while. Then apply a strong, steady pull with your tools. Be aware that tools can slip off and hurt your hands badly. Blood and bad words usually follow.

If additional leverage is needed

TRAIL REPAIRS

Hopefully, being towed out of a trail does not become a regular experience. However, doing it right will save friendships and damage to your vehicles. Try to follow the path of the truck that is doing the towing and try not to create too much drag when being pulled. The exception may be when stopping. Gently apply the brakes before the tow vehicle so that the tow strap remains taut. Otherwise, you'll have a bungee effect, and it can be awkward. Practice makes perfect, or at least it won't be as ugly.

to remove a stubborn nut, carry a longer steel pipe that will slide over the breaker bar handle. You may even want to carry a small MAP-Pro gas torch like plumbers use to solder copper pipes. Applying heat to a nut will cause it to expand slightly, and that may be enough to release its grip.

A bar of soap rubbed on a crack can seal a plastic gas tank. There are also epoxy products available to seal plastic gas tanks and radiator tanks.

Trail Towing

If you are being towed on a trail, try to follow the path of the tow vehicle. If the engine is off, that may require some significant strength to turn the steering wheel. Make sure that the steering column is unlocked. Anticipate slowing or stopping by dragging the brakes a little to keep the tow strap taut and not hit the vehicle that is towing you. Without power brakes, it is necessary to plan ahead. With practice, you will get better at this skill.

Once at a safe place to park at a trailhead or paved road, figure out how to get your truck or SUV home or to the nearest repair shop. Does someone in the group have a truck and trailer? Can a tow truck reach you and tow your truck to town? Having a AAA membership can come in handy if you think you might need towing services.

Finally, life is about making memories and having campfire stories. Some will be good, and others will be bad. In the end, it is better to have memorable experiences than to not. Who wants to sit in a nursing home one day with no stories to tell?

CHAPTER 11

COMMUNICATION

Being able to speak with other people on the trail can be fun, but it can also be very important. In addition, on rare occasions, it can be lifesaving. Most of the time, speaking with others helps everyone know what's happening: "Turn left up here at the next intersection." "Be careful at this obstacle; the best path is on the right." "Let's have lunch up here by the waterfall."

We are lucky to have so many means of communicating on the trail now. Technology keeps getting better. We have family radio service (FRS) radios, general mobile radio service (GMRS) radios, multiple-use radio service (MURS) radios, CB (citizens band) radios, and ham radios. We also have satellite devices that pair with your cell phone, stand-alone satellite phones, and finally, as a last resort, personal locator beacons. Each has its place and comes at a cost.

Ironically, cellular phones are the worst way to talk among a group when off-road. Cell phones are really designed for speaking one to one. Conference calls on the trail aren't practical. In addition, cellular coverage deteriorates quickly once you leave paved roads. Most towers are placed where there are towns or traffic.

Frequency Ranges

The three frequency ranges that are used for the majority of communication are high frequency (HF), very high frequency (VHF), and ultra high frequency (UHF).

HF frequencies are between 3 and 30 MHz, and they are much more affected by atmospheric and electronics interference. CB radios operate within the HF band at about 27 MHz. One drawback of using the HF frequencies is that antennas need to be relatively large to be effective.

VHF frequencies range from 30 to 300 MHz. This band is desirable due to its short-distance propagation. VHF and higher frequencies usually are not reflected by the

Having some form of communication when driving off-road is important. It may be a simple way to talk among a small group of fellow drivers or it can be a way to summon help in an emergency.

128   THE ULTIMATE OFF-ROAD DRIVER'S GUIDE

COMMUNICATION

Some of the communication options go far beyond a simple handheld radio. Satellite-based devices can track your location with their global positioning system (GPS) and let friends and family know where you are and that you are okay. (Photo Courtesy Nicole Glass Photography/Shutterstock.com)

ionosphere and are perfect for navigation systems and weather stations. These frequencies and above are considered "line of sight" because they do not extend beyond the horizon.

UHF acts much the same as VHF with the benefit of having a physically short wavelength, so the size of equipment, such as antennas, can be kept very small. UHF frequencies range from between 300 MHz and 3 GHz.

One of the challenges that we face is deciding which type of radio to buy and use. In many cases, that depends on with whom you are communicating. 4WD clubs and

List of FRS Channels Compared to GMRS			
Channel	Frequency (MHz)	FRS Power Restriction	GMRS Power Restriction
1	462.5625	Up to 2 watts	Up to 5 watts
2	462.5875	Up to 2 watts	Up to 5 watts
3	462.6125	Up to 2 watts	Up to 5 watts
4	462.6375	Up to 2 watts	Up to 5 watts
5	462.6625	Up to 2 watts	Up to 5 watts
6	462.6875	Up to 2 watts	Up to 5 watts
7	462.7125	Up to 2 watts	Up to 5 watts
8	467.5625	Up to 0.5 watt	Up to 0.5 watt
9	467.5875	Up to 0.5 watt	Up to 0.5 watt
10	467.6125	Up to 0.5 watt	Up to 0.5 watt
11	467.6375	Up to 0.5 watt	Up to 0.5 watt
12	467.6625	Up to 0.5 watt	Up to 0.5 watt
13	467.6875	Up to 0.5 watt	Up to 0.5 watt
14	467.7125	Up to 0.5 watt	Up to 0.5 watt
15	462.5500	Up to 2 watts	Up to 50 watts
16	462.5750	Up to 2 watts	Up to 50 watts
17	462.6000	Up to 2 watts	Up to 50 watts
18	462.6250	Up to 2 watts	Up to 50 watts
19	462.6500	Up to 2 watts	Up to 50 watts
20	462.6750	Up to 2 watts	Up to 50 watts
21	462.7000	Up to 2 watts	Up to 50 watts
22	462.7250	Up to 2 watts	Up to 50 watts

FRS and GMRS radios use the same frequencies but can transmit at different power on some of them (specifically channels 1–7 and 15–22).

organized events may have standardized a CB or GMRS radio. However, if you travel alone and want to update folks back home on your location, a satellite-based device might be better.

One day, we may look back and laugh when all of these devices are as obsolete as a payphone. However, for now, we will use what we have.

FRS Radios

Let's talk about FRS radios first. FRS radios are an inexpensive walkie-talkie with limited power and range. The antenna is small and built in. They are limited to 2 watts of power, but most FRS-only radios actually transmit at 0.5 watt.

Some people use them because they are cheap and easy to use. They will work as long as you are close to each other. The range that is advertised has been tested under ideal conditions. In the real world, expect a range of 0.3 to 1 mile, depending on the terrain.

FRS radios frequently use inaudible tone squelch codes to filter out unwanted conversations from other users on the same frequency. Although these squelch codes are sometimes called privacy codes or private line (PL) codes, they offer no protection from eavesdropping and are only intended to help reduce unwanted chatter when sharing busy channels.

The FCC limits the FRS frequencies from between 462 and 467 MHz. This is done so that they don't overlap with other types of radios.

GMRS radios are replacing CB radios among off-road drivers. They can transmit with up to 50 watts of power, and the range is up to 15 miles, depending on the terrain.

FRS radios are commonly found, affordable, and easy to use. They have small antennas and limited power, so they are only useful with small groups that travel close together. There are no FCC tests or licenses needed and no monthly subscription fees.

GMRS Radios

GMRS radios have been around since the 1960s, but their advantages are causing them to become more popular now. They outperform CB radios because their audio is clearer, and they can transmit and receive farther than a typical CB radio. However, they also cost two to three times that of a CB radio.

GMRS radios also operate within the 462 to 467 MHz range and have designated channels within those frequencies that aren't available to FRS radios. They do require an FCC license, but there is no test. The license is good for 10 years and covers immediate family members too. The license fee at this time is $35.

GMRS radios can transmit with up to 50 watts of power and typically transmit/receive up to 15 miles in real-world conditions, depending on the terrain. Higher power does not necessarily provide greater range, although it may be more reliable at the limits of line-of-sight distance.

Reaching Out

A GMRS radio's range can be expanded exponentially with the use of repeaters. Repeaters are similar to the cell phone towers that are placed all around the country.

The way repeaters work is that instead of a GMRS signal going directly from one radio to another, the signal is sent to the repeater and then forwarded on to the intended radio receiver. This repeater service increases the range dramatically, with

COMMUNICATION

A MURS radio is a step up from an FRS radio because it transmits at 2 watts of power instead of 0.5 watts. However, of course, it costs more. The real challenge is that the other drivers who you want to communicate with will need to have MURS radios too. MURS radios are not commonly found in the off-road community. (Photo Courtesy Offroad Communications)

Garmin offers a unique device that combines a MURS radio with a GPS map display. This device allows you to track other drivers on the GPS map display and to talk with them via the MURS radio. The primary challenge is that the other drivers need to have the same device for the tracking to work. (Photo Courtesy Offroad Communications)

each individual repeater being able to send out signals up to a 20-mile diameter around it. The range for GMRS radios can be increased to hundreds of miles when using multiple repeaters.

Be aware that repeaters are privately owned, and you'll need to ask permission to use them. Some repeaters are simply not listed.

Squelch

When listening to people on your trail ride or group on a GMRS radio, you may hear other conversations on the same channel. This happens most often where there are a number of OHV people using the same GMRS channels that you are.

With a CB radio, you adjust the squelch knob to reduce static or unwanted conversations. Squelch filters out weaker signals, letting you focus on the stronger signals near you. FRS radio manufacturers call this privacy codes. A filter only lets people on the same privacy code hear each other.

GMRS, HF, and UHF radios all have a similar function called tone squelch. Continuous tone-coded squelch system (CTCSS) and digital code squelch (DCS) are forms of tone squelch. They use an inaudible data stream that is passed along with the transmission. This inaudible data stream filters out unwanted conversations and static. CTCSS circuitry mutes those users who are using a different CTCSS tone or no CTCSS at all.

Digital code squelch (DCS) is a more recent version of tone squelch that adds more codes, but also requires more bandwidth.

MURS Radios

MURS uses five channels in the 151- to 154-MHz range. Transmitter power is limited to 2 watts. The most common use of MURS radios is for short-distance, two-way communications using small, portable handheld radios that function similar to FRS walkie-talkies. The primary advantage of a MURS radio is that it transmits

Frequencies		
Channel	Frequency	Name
1	151.82 MHz	MURS 1
2	151.88 MHz	MURS 2
3	151.94 MHz	MURS 3
4	154.57 MHz	Blue Dot
5	154.60 MHz	Green Dot
There are only five frequencies (channels) assigned to MURS radios. Being limited by the FCC to 2 watts of transmitting power and not being allowed to use repeaters limits range to about 1 to 1.5 miles for normal use.		

at 2 watts of power and therefore has greater range than an FRS radio.

MURS range varies, depending on antenna size and placement. Typically, users will get a range of 1 to 1.5 miles. MURS uses five channels that were previously in the industrial/business radio service.

Established by the FCC in the fall of 2000, no FCC license is needed and the use of repeaters is not allowed.

An interesting device is now on the market. It is manufactured by Garmin, and it combines a MURS radio and a GPS display with map overlays. Up to 20 other Tread users are displayed on the GPS map, making it possible to keep track of fellow drivers and to talk to them.

CB Radios

Citizens band (CB) radios came out in 1948 and were all the rage in the 1970s. People had base stations at home, truck drivers used them extensively and modified them, and popular songs were written about them. Betty Ford, the former First Lady of the United States, used the CB handle "First Mama."

CB transmitting power is limited to 4 watts in the United States, and it has a range of between 3 miles and 20 miles, depending on the terrain. CB radios operate on 40 channels near 27 MHz in the high frequency (a.k.a. shortwave) band. The citizens band frequencies are distinct from other radios, such as FRS, GMRS, MURS, and the amateur radio service (ham radio).

Channel 9 was officially reserved for emergency use by the FCC in 1969. Many CBers call channel 19 "the trucker's channel." It is the standard channel that truck drivers use to communicate with each other.

Virtually all 4WD clubs and events have used CB radios as the standard for the last 50 years, and some still do. CB radios are commonly available, affordable, and don't require an FCC license.

CB radios have been around for more than 70 years. They were commonly found among off-road drivers and truck drivers. The general public joined in during the 1970s, but the craze eventually faded away. Truckers still have them, and many old-school four-wheelers have them too. For a while, it seemed as though everyone had a CB. (Photo Courtesy Virrage Images/Shutterstock.com)

CB radio users have agreed that Channel 9 is reserved for emergencies and that Channel 19 is the standard channel that truck drivers use. It can be useful to listen in on Channel 19 if you are stuck in traffic on an interstate highway due to an accident or construction.

COMMUNICATION

CB Radio Channels	
Channel	Frequency (MHz)
1	26.965
2	26.975
3	26.985
4	27.005
5	27.015
6	27.025
7	27.035
8	27.055
9	27.065
10	27.075
11	27.085
12	27.105
13	27.115
14	27.125
15	27.135
16	27.155
17	27.165
18	27.175
19	27.185
20	27.205
21	27.215
22	27.225
23	27.255
24	27.235
25	27.245
26	27.265
27	27.275
28	27.285
29	27.295
30	27.305
31	27.315
32	27.325
33	27.335
34	27.345
35	27.355
36	27.365
37	27.375
38	27.385
39	27.395
40	27.405

Most CB radios sold in the United States have the following features:

Squelch	A specialized type of filter designed to suppress static and weak signals
CB/WX switch	Selects between CB radio or NOAA weather stations
PA	Some transceivers can drive an external speaker and act as a low-power bullhorn
RF gain	Adjusts the RF amplifier gain of the receiver to reduce background noise
SWR	A meter used to monitor reflected power caused by mismatched antennas and cables
Automatic level control (ALC)	Limits the transmitter modulation level to reduce distortion
Automatic noise limiter (ANL)	Reduces background noise (such as ignition spark)
Microphone gain (Dynamike)	Controls how loud you sound to everyone else

CB radios are preprogrammed by the manufacturer and typically just show the channel number, not the frequency. There are 40 channels available to CB radio users.

THE ULTIMATE OFF-ROAD DRIVER'S GUIDE

Ham Radio

It is important to note that the term "ham radio" does not describe any particular radio or frequency range (known as a band). Ham radio is also known as "amateur radio."

Having a ham radio license from the FCC allows you to use a great number of radio frequencies set aside specifically for recreation and public service use. These are at significantly higher power levels than those that are available to CB users (up to 1,500 watts in the United States).

To become a ham radio operator, you must pass a test. The good news is that knowing Morse code is no longer a requirement for any amateur radio service class. There are three different licenses that grant an applicant access to different frequency ranges (bands).

The first ham license is called the technician class license. For most recreational users, the technician class license is enough. It allows you to transmit at up to 200 watts on HF bands and provides access to the most common VHF and UHF frequencies. The technician class licensing exam consists of multiple-choice questions. It can usually be passed after studying one of the study-guide books that are widely available.

The next level of access is available with a general license. With a general license, you can transmit at up to 1,500 watts and have access to even more frequency bands. This license is needed for emergency communications. You can also access the Winlink email system and send voice over HF. This test is a bit harder, but once you pass, you have greater privileges.

The highest level of license is the extra license. It is aptly named because it gives you access to the

Use of a ham radio requires passing an FCC test and paying a modest license fee. In the past, a Morse code test was required, but that has been dropped for several years. Ham radios can transmit at up to 1,500 watts and can communicate around the world through the use of repeaters. These powerful radios are often used for public service to help communicate and coordinate relief during disasters. Among the off-road community, you will find them being used most often in western states with vast unpopulated areas. (Photo Courtesy Lisa F. Young/Shutterstock.com)

The use of repeaters greatly extends the effective range for ham radio operators. It is one of the advantages that the FCC has allowed for these radios. Volunteers place repeaters at high elevations on towers or buildings to allow ham radio operators to better communicate. A radio repeater is a device that receives a low-level radio signal and retransmits it at a higher power so that the signal can cover longer distances with greater clarity. (Photo Courtesy Dmitry Gladkov/Shutterstock.com)

most amateur HF bands. Typically, only avid ham radio enthusiasts get this level of license.

Ham radios allow us to communicate with others at significant distances. One of the great benefits of ham radio is the access to repeaters. A repeater is simply a radio device that receives a radio signal and retransmits it farther along. Repeaters sit atop mountains or towers, and there are thousands of them scattered worldwide.

For amateur radio, the vast majority of these repeaters are free to use. As the repeaters are situated high above the surrounding terrain, it is possible for them to reach an area sometimes hundreds of miles in diameter, making the lowest-powered personal radio become one of the highest powered.

Satellites

While the use of radios works pretty well from one person to another, the radio waves travel horizontally by line of sight. Mountains, buildings, or other tall obstacles can interfere with communication. Usually, that interference is seen as reduced range.

There are a small number of satellite networks orbiting overhead, and more are coming. We have satellite radio, GPS, TV, and internet. Satellite phone networks exist, but the phones and monthly fees can get expensive.

Satellite networks are the key to staying connected no matter where you go. Satellite phones and other communication solutions use one of two types of networks.

Networks

The first type, low earth orbit (LEO) networks, are made up of multiple satellites orbiting earth at an altitude of 1,000 miles or less. Iridium, Inmarsat, Globalstar, and someday SpaceX use LEO networks.

The second type is known as a geosynchronus orbit (GEO) network. With this type of network, satellites are placed at a higher altitude that is usually about 22,000 miles above earth and lined up along the equator. They orbit at the same speed of earth's rotation, essentially keeping them stationary.

The type of network that's right for you depends on your needs. But the key is that your satellite phone antenna must have a direct view to the sky for it to work. Heavily wooded trails can block the overhead signal, but open areas are ideal. In most cases, you can drive or walk to an open area to get a signal. When the satellite phone connects with a satellite overhead, you will have a crystal-clear call almost anywhere in the world.

Regardless of which satellite network provider you choose, having a stand-alone phone is an important and expensive part of the solution. Many satellite phone users are employees working in remote areas beyond cell phone coverage.

An interesting satellite-based device is available from Garmin that is not a phone, but it connects a cellular phone to the Iridium network and allows two-way texting/emails, emergency SOS messages, GPS tracking, location sharing, and optional

CHAPTER 11

Satellite Network Providers		
Provider	**Orbit Type**	**Number of Satellites**
Globalstar	Low earth orbit	32
Inmarsat	Geosynchronous	3
Iridium	Low earth orbit	66

weather forecasts. It is called InReach.

A similar device from Globalstar connects its SPOT X satellite device to your smartphone via Bluetooth and uses an app to send texts, emails, or social media posts from your phone. It also supports SOS messages, GPS tracking, and location sharing.

Naturally, a monthly satellite subscription is required for both devices.

Emergencies

In an emergency, you can trigger a personal locator beacon (PLB) that sends a coded SOS message on the 406 MHz distress frequency. That message is relayed to the nearest rescuers, who can follow the 121.5 MHz homing signal to find your exact location. Some units have a bright strobe light to help rescuers see you once they get close.

PLBs are designed to be used anywhere in the world. Once activated, they will transmit for a minimum of 24 hours. The battery life in storage is usually six years. The battery can be tested during storage to verify that it is working. There is no subscription required.

Be aware that emergency position indicator radio beacons (EPIRBs) may be advertised as emergency beacons. Marine EPIRBs are different than PLBs. EPIRBs are intended for use on boats, but PLBs are for personal use and can legally be used on land by outdoor enthusiasts.

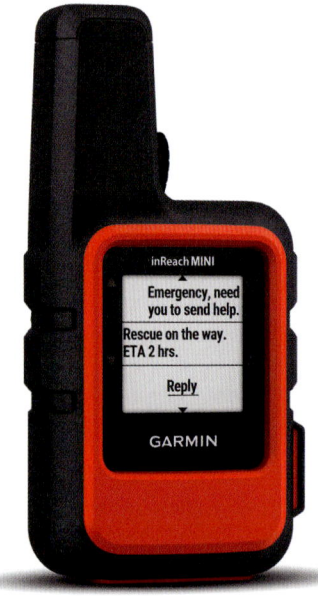

Satellite networks have either low earth orbits or geosynchronous earth orbits. Each has its advantage regarding coverage. The primary advantage of using satellite networks is that the signal is beamed up, not horizontally using line of sight. As long as you have a fairly clear view of the sky, your device should be able to reach a satellite. Once you do, that signal can be beamed back down anywhere in the world. (Photo Courtesy Offroad Communications)

With some satellite-based devices, you can connect your cellular phone to a satellite network and have two-way texting/emails, emergency SOS messages, GPS tracking, location sharing, and weather forecasts. (Photo Courtesy Offroad Communications)

CHAPTER 12

NAVIGATION

One of the greatest fears that people have is getting lost. Well, that's after their fear of spiders . . . or heights . . . or the dark. Daniel Boone once famously said, "I have never been lost, but I will admit to being confused for several weeks."

Luckily for us, most of the United States has been explored and mapped by the pioneers and Google. Our challenge today is to select what type of navigation system to use and how large the display should be. There are endless mapping apps and software choices.

We all have similar goals. We want to see where we are, where we want to go, and how to get there.

Navigating on the streets and highways of America is pretty straightforward. The maps are good, but they need to be updated periodically due to the endless construction projects. Just follow the orange barrels.

When we leave pavement, the street signs go away, and the orange barrels disappear. Your GPS may just display blank areas. So, now what?

Topographic Maps

The most basic paper map typically used for off-road travel is the topographical (topo) map. Topo maps show the contours of the land (topography), roads, and many landmarks. These maps are created by the US Geological Survey (USGS). The USGS has been making topo maps for 130 years.

The USGS has divided the United States into smaller grids that are known as quadrangles. This makes the maps a manageable size and scale. For practice, look up the topo map for your home or familiar trails online. Use an internet search engine and type in "USGS Map Locator."

Once at that website, scroll the cursor around the national map to find your state and area. Zoom in

The key to avoid getting lost is preparation. Chapter 1 will help you prepare for your trail ride, and Chapter 12 will help ensure that you have what you need to navigate your way through your trip. There are very few places in the United States that are unmapped. Please stay on the roads and trails to travel safely. (Photo Courtesy Air Images/Shutterstock.com)

THE ULTIMATE OFF-ROAD DRIVER'S GUIDE

and out to see the names for each quadrangle. With the name of the quadrangle, you can download it or order the map that you want.

These maps can be downloaded from the USGS website for free. Printed topo maps can be purchased from the USGS store.

Once you see a familiar quad, study the roads, trails, and landmarks that the map shows. It's an easy way to learn what these maps offer.

The wavy lines on these maps are known as the contour intervals, and they show elevation changes. Lines that are close together indicate steep terrain. That could be a mountain or a valley. Wider contour lines indicate more gradual changes, such as gently rolling hills.

On the edges of the USGS maps, there is information about when the map was last updated, the various symbols, and a lot more.

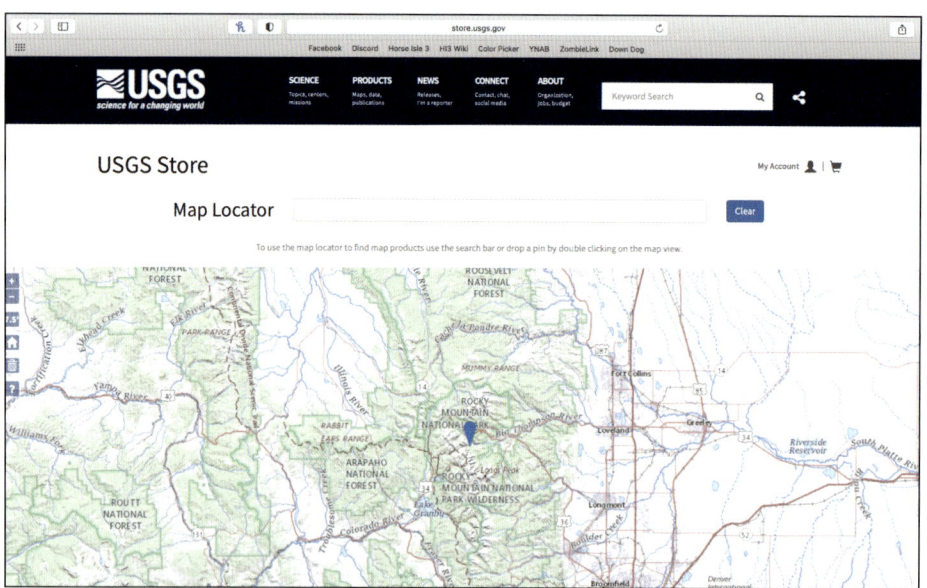

The earth is not flat, so topography maps show the hills and valleys. The roads, trails, and landmarks make them a useful source of information when driving off-road. The entire country has been mapped by the USGS and then divided into quadrangles to provide them in a manageable size and scale. Go to store.usgs.gov/map-locator for more information.

USGS topographic maps are in 1:24,000 scale, and are also known as 7.5-minute quadrangles. From approximately 1947 to 1992, more than 55,000 printed 7.5-minute maps were made to cover the 48 lower states. Alaska and Hawaii were mapped in different scales. Now, these maps are published digitally using GIS data and are known as "US Topo" maps. Go to natgeomaps.com/trail-maps/pdf-quads for more information.

A Map and Compass

People have been using a map and compass for a very long time. It was a common skill back in the days before GPS devices and cell phones. Map reading and compass navigation were taught to young people in the Boy Scouts and Girl Scouts. This was a common subject at summer camps.

Even today, there are rallies and other timed events that rely exclusively on the use of maps and a compass.

Traveling off-road usually means following dirt roads or trails. Some are well marked, but others are not. There are a variety of paper maps and digital devices that will allow you to find your location and let you see the path forward to your destination.

For cross-country travel in vast, wide-open areas, using a map and compass will show the most direct route to your destination. An online search will show a lot of books and websites that will teach you how to

NAVIGATION

The contour intervals are helpful in knowing how steep the terrain is. The landmarks are great because they help locate you on the map. Although, the GPS coordinates along the edge of the map do that too. Trails, dirt roads, and paved roads are also shown. The legend at the bottom of the map has interesting information. (Photo Courtesy Jeff Metzger/Shutterstock.com)

Paper maps and a compass are still relevant today. They are simple to use and reliable. There are a variety of rallies that only allow map and compass navigation. The Rebelle Rally is one example in the United States. Online training and classes are commonly available. (Photo Courtesy Rebelle Rally)

use a map and compass. Some specialized sporting goods stores or co-ops sell compasses and offer in-person classes on how to use them.

DeLorme Atlas and Gazetteer Paper Maps

A step up for off-road use may be the DeLorme Atlas & Gazetteer paper maps. These atlases are available for all 50 states. They are based on the topo map quadrangles, and they include dirt roads, trails, campgrounds, and other useful information for outdoor enthusiasts. They are sold online and at sporting goods stores. They are a large format 11 x 15.5-inch paper atlas.

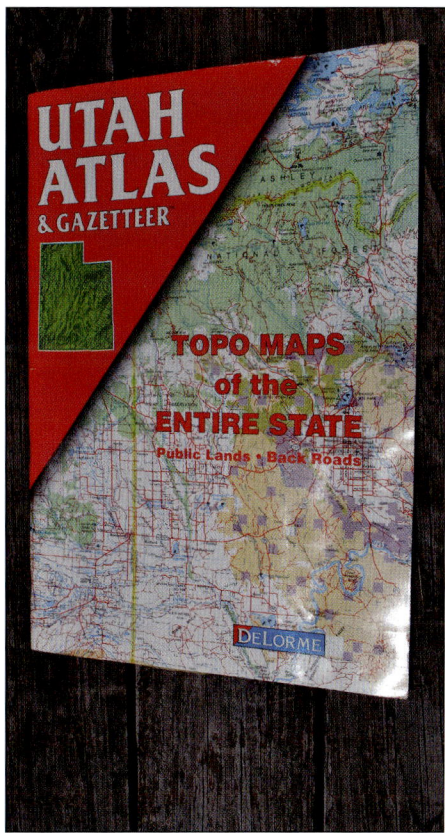

The DeLorme Atlas has been a staple in the off-road community for many years. Founded in 1976, its popularity began before digital maps became available.

THE ULTIMATE OFF-ROAD DRIVER'S GUIDE

CHAPTER 12

Printable MVUMs

Federal agencies, such as the US Forest Service (USFS) and Bureau of Land Management (BLM), are required to publish their motor vehicle use maps (MVUMs) for all roads and trails that are available for use within their jurisdiction. These maps are required to be updated annually.

"MVUMs are a requirement of the Travel Management Rule and reflect travel management decisions on each National Forest and National Grassland," according to the US Forest Service. "The MVUM is a black-and-white map with no topographic features. It is not a stand-alone map, and is best used along with a forest visitor map or other topographic map. The MVUM displays National Forest System (NFS) routes (roads and trails) or areas designated open to motorized travel.

"The MVUM also displays [the] allowed uses by vehicle class (highway-legal vehicles, vehicles less

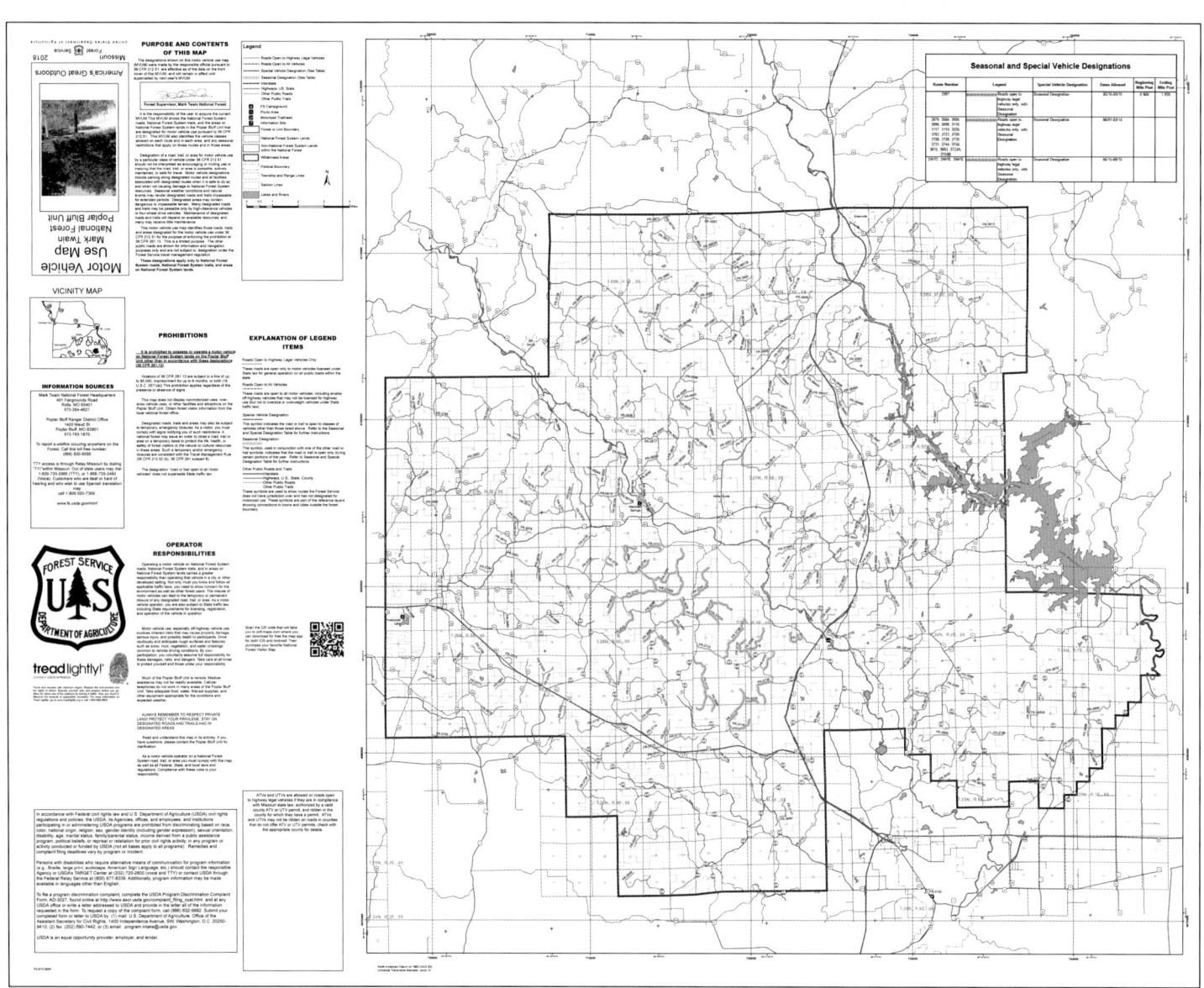

Motor vehicle use maps (MVUM) can be printed on a large-scale printer, but they are most often downloaded into a GPS device to provide a map layer that shows the legal roads and trails within public lands managed by a federal agency—usually, the US Forest Service (USFS) or Bureau of Land Management (BLM). Keep in mind that these maps don't show temporary or seasonal closures due to hunting seasons, controlled burns, wildfires, or maintenance. It's best to call the local USFS or BLM office and ask about current closures and road/trail conditions. Heavy rains can make some roads or trails impassable.

NAVIGATION

than 50 inches wide, and motorcycles), seasonal allowances, and other travel rule and regulation information. Routes not shown on the MVUM are not open to public motor vehicle travel. Routes designated for motorized use may not always be signed on the ground but will be identified on the MVUM.

"The public is responsible for referencing the MVUM to determine designated routes for motor vehicle use. MVUMs will be updated annually to correct mapping errors or discrepancies and update travel decisions."

MVUM maps are sometimes incorporated into digital map apps as an additional layer.

These maps are very important for travel on public lands. They tell you whether you are on a legal road/trail or not.

Guidebooks

Some areas have well-known trails that are popular with both locals and tourists. This is especially true in some Western US towns. Printed guidebooks can be found in local souvenir shops and visitor centers. They offer a wealth of information about trail locations, GPS coordinates, trail difficulty, time frames to run the trail, scenic spots, and much more.

Their primary downside is that they can become outdated quickly as the trails age and change. Land management agencies open and close trails, and weather can significantly change the difficulty level.

With that being said, they are a good reference. A good source of current trail conditions can be Jeep rental businesses. They often provide guided tours too. So, they are usually familiar with the local trails and can offer good advice.

Google Maps and Google Earth

When leaving paved roads and towns, it doesn't take long before cell

Guidebooks are an easy way to see popular trails in tourist areas. When folks from out of town arrive and decide to rent a 4WD for the day or use their own to see local trails, guidebooks can be a good option. Typically, the passenger navigates by reading the book as the driver drives. It's simple and requires no technology. The only real downside is that any book will become inaccurate or obsolete over time. It is hard to keep them updated. They are a snapshot in the time in which they were written.

Although the Google Maps app uses GPS signals to find your location, it relies on cellular data to provide all the extra features it is known for. It excels along roads and towns where cellular coverage is good.

THE ULTIMATE OFF-ROAD DRIVER'S GUIDE

CHAPTER 12

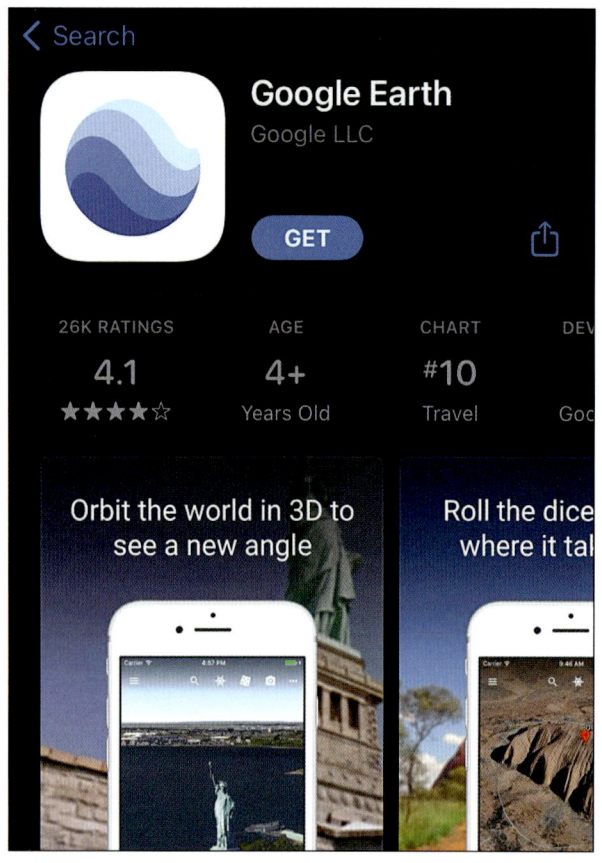

The Google Earth app is a subset of Google Maps. It uses GPS signals to locate you and display satellite images. It still has some points of interest but does not have all of the features that are found in Maps. It is an excellent tool for pre-trip planning.

phone coverage weakens and then disappears. Luckily, Google uses GPS signals to pinpoint your location on a digital map. However, the Google Maps app uses cellular data for extra features, such as traffic reporting, points of interest (POI), and route planning. As a result, Google Maps doesn't function very well without access to cellular data.

Google Maps does allow you to download map data while you have cellular or Wi-Fi access to be used later when you don't. This offline map can be paired with your device's GPS function to see where you are and the surrounding area. These offline maps are available to you for one year.

Google Earth, on the other hand, is a more GPS-focused subset of Google Maps with much more detailed satellite imagery. It doesn't clutter up the imagery with turn-by-turn navigation and traffic reports. It can be useful for online exploration and planning before you go off-road. You can "fly" above the trail and follow it from beginning to end.

If you download good maps into your phone, tablet, or GPS at home, you can track and record where you

Automotive manufacturers usually watch and wait to see what trends are occurring before adding them to their cars and trucks. So, for a while we had a satellite radio receiver stuck on the windshield with a suction cup. Then, we added a portable GPS unit, cell phone mounts, and so forth. Eventually, manufacturers started adding larger displays in the dash that had Sirius XM satellite radio capability, GPS navigation, Bluetooth cellular communication, and more. Cellular Wi-Fi is available in some new cars too.

NAVIGATION

Having good maps is essential, but being able to see what you need in an easy-to-use device is important too, especially as you bounce along a rough dirt road or trail. Tiny buttons or complex menus can ruin your experience. Easy, intuitive devices win in the consumer market. (Photo Courtesy mariakray/Shutterstock.com)

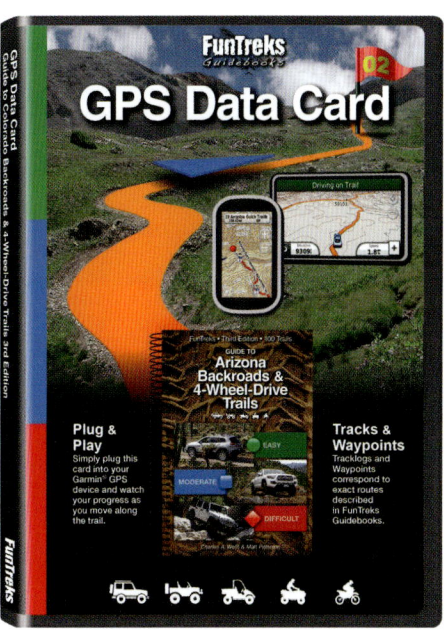

The ability to buy digital maps on an SD card is great. We can buy the maps that we need and create layers. Combining basic topographical maps, open street maps, and MVUMs is a good start. If using private OHV parks, add in those trails as needed. (Photo Courtesy FunTreks Guidebooks)

are located using the GPS function in the unit, rather than cellular data.

GPS

There are a crazy number of GPS devices available to display digital maps. Some are built into the dash by the car's manufacturer, and aftermarket options can be purchased and stuck on the windshield with a suction cup.

Serious map users may have larger displays mounted on a rail system in front of the dash (and airbags). Digital maps for off-road use may need to display large areas, and so a larger display can be easier to use. However, in some cases, the dash becomes cluttered with radios and displays. This can be a distraction and can affect your visibility outside.

The key to successful navigation off-road is to have good maps. Google has done a pretty thorough job of mapping streets, but very little has been mapped on dirt trails. Naturally, maps are improved each year, and it pays dividends to update your maps periodically, especially if you are going into unfamiliar areas.

The market has exploded for digital maps and the devices that display them. Your experience with these devices will vary based on their functionality. Some are awesome, and some are awkward. You'll need to do some research, and maybe you can find someone who actually has the unit you want. Personal experience is always better than advice from a keyboard expert.

No matter how big the display is or how many features the device has, the quality and accuracy of the maps are what matters. Digital maps that are in a GPS exchange format (.gpx) file format can be bought and loaded into your GPS device on an SD card.

GPS exchange format is a common XML data format that can be used to store waypoints, tracks, and routes. A waypoint is any single specific location. A route is a sequence of waypoints. It's the plan for your navigation. A track is the recorded path that you actually followed at the end of the day.

Digital maps may also include points of interest (POI). The format is open, and there are no licensing fees. Location data is stored in tags and can be interchanged between GPS devices and map software. Digital map apps can be bought for your phone or tablet through the Google Play Store or Apple's App Store.

Additional maps can be bought online and downloaded into a

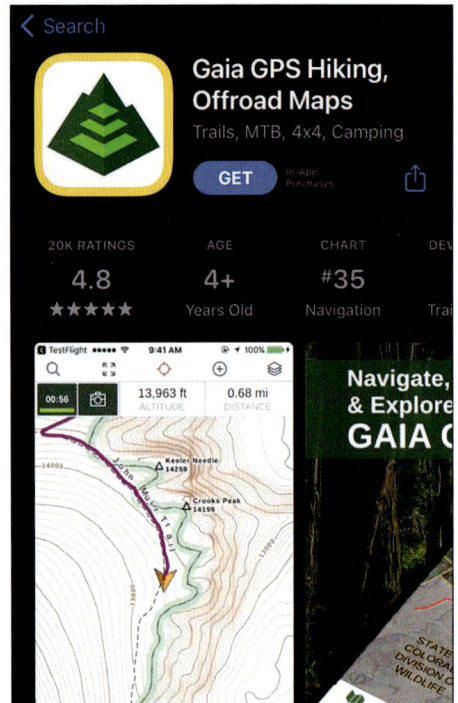

Mapping apps, such as GAIA and Backcountry Navigator, can be downloaded and used for off-road navigation. They reside on your phone, tablet, or GPS device and are updated periodically.

Private OHV park owners have long struggled to produce and update paper maps. In addition, people keep the old maps and don't want to pay for new ones again and again. One solution is to have a map contractor make an initial map or app and then update it as needed. This solution allows OHV drivers to update their digital maps periodically.

Polaris's Ride Command app relies on cellular service to display where other drivers are located. This is a downside because we often drive beyond cellular networks. However, Garmin's Tread Group Ride Radio feature can help keep track of up to 20 drivers using the integrated MURS radio. However, the other drivers must use the same Tread system for the tracking to work. Watch for this trend to evolve and solve these limitations. (Photo Courtesy Offroad Communications)

dedicated GPS device. For example, adding the MVUM maps as a layer is a good idea if you will be using roads or trails on public lands.

iOverlander is a popular app with all kinds of POI data added by the software's users. GAIA, Backcountry Navigator, and OnX are popular for now.

Google Maps and Google Earth were mentioned earlier. Open Street Maps is a similar product that is free and very accurate. The list of map apps is truly endless with people who either love them or hate them.

One thing to look for when considering your purchases is where map companies get their data. Do they create it themselves or do they rely on their customers to add it for them? For example, iOverlander is a nonprofit project primarily run by volunteers. It has developed a large community of people contributing data, and it is well regarded. However, some large corporations have launched similar online mapping projects only to have them fail due to a lack of participation and accuracy.

There are some companies that offer maps specifically for off-road trails in particular areas. Their maps show the trails in private OHV parks or on state recreational trails. Examples of these map sources are CartoTracks and Lifetime Trailmaps. Of course, there are others, and all of these companies are working hard to add to their library of maps.

The UTV market is driving some unique products that allow the tracking of other drivers in your group. So, if your trail ride gets split up or spread out, you can see the location of each driver on the map. However, be aware that the tracking may require a cellular signal or special radio to work.